MENTORING
The Strategy
Of The
Master

Also by Ron Lee Davis:

Gold in the Making
A Forgiving God in an Unforgiving World
Healing Life's Hurts
A Time for Compassion
Courage to Begin Again
Mistreated
Becoming a Whole Person in a Broken World

MENTORING
The Strategy Of The Master

by
Ron Lee Davis
with
James D. Denney

THOMAS NELSON PUBLISHERS
Nashville

❖ *A Janet Thoma Book* ❖

Published in Nashville, Tennessee, by Thomas Nelson, Inc., and distributed
in Canada by Lawson Falle, Ltd., Cambridge, Ontario.

Printed in the United States of America.

Unless otherwise noted, Scripture quotations are from the NEW KING JAMES
VERSION of the Bible. Copyright © 1979, 1980, 1982, Thomas Nelson
Publishers, Inc.

Scripture quotations noted NIV are from The Holy Bible: NEW
INTERNATIONAL VERSION. Copyright © 1978 by the New York
International Bible Society. Used by permission of Zondervan Bible Publishers.

Library of Congress Cataloging-in-Publication Data

Davis, Ron Lee.
    Mentoring : the strategy of the Master / Ron Lee Davis with James
D. Denney.
      p.   cm.
    Includes bibliographical references.
    ISBN 0-8407-7195-9
    1. Witness bearing (Christianity) 2. Christian life—1960-
I. Denney, James D. II. Title.
BV4520.D38   1991
253—dc20   90-25907
                                          CIP

Printed in the United States of America
1 2 3 4 5 6 7 — 96 95 94 93 92 91

Dedicated to my son Nathan
who constantly challenges me by his
compassion, courage, sensitivity, and love
to seek to become a better mentor.

I love you, Nathan.

"My son, you and I will always be together."
Luke 15:31

CONTENTS

Part One:

THE
ONE-ON-ONE
RELATIONSHIP

Chapter 1

LIVING FOR THE NEXT GENERATION

*More time spent with
fewer people . . .*

THE HEART OF A CARPENTER

Aside from my own father, the most pivotal mentor in my life has been a man named Dean Frost. Dean never earned a Ph.D., ran a corporation, wrote a book, or was listed in *Who's Who*. The man I consider the most important mentor in my young adult life was a carpenter in a little Iowa town called Mt. Ayr.

When I first met Dean Frost, I was twenty-one and he was in his late thirties. I had come to be the pastor of the sixty-member Mt. Ayr Presbyterian Church, where Dean was an elder. Before I came, this little church had been without a pastor for more than two years and was struggling to decide whether or not to close its doors. With my arrival, they at last had a pastor—of sorts. More precisely, they had a seminary student who commuted 700 miles round-trip between school and a three-day-a-week job at the church. (Clearly, these were desperate folks, and they would take whatever they could get, even a pastor-in-training with just one semester of seminary between his ears.)

I received quite an education in that little church, especially as I lived and worked alongside Dean, a man of unpretentious faith and deep Christian character. My education took place over the dozens of home-cooked meals I shared in the home of Dean and his wife, Louise, and during many long after-dinner talks I had with him in his living room.

Dean was always available to me and his home was always open. He took the time to invest in my life. When we talked together, there was seldom any agenda. We just shared deeply from our own spiritual walk with Christ, from our own struggles and joys in trying to become more like Jesus.

I especially remember one Sunday when Dean and I drove out to Mt. Ayr Lake, about three miles out of town. We had often gone out to the lake with our youth group or for the church picnic. But on this particular trip, we went alone. Dean was troubled.

It was late afternoon when we pulled up to the lakeshore. A light breeze ruffled the water and stirred the pine trees that ringed the lake. We went out on the dock and sat with our backs against the rail and looked out over the water. "I've been worried about Janet and Mark," he said, referring to two teenagers, sister and brother, who were in our church youth group. "They're living with their stepmother right now, but their natural parents don't want them to live there. Our family's been discussing the possibility of taking them into our home."

"For how long?" I asked.

"For good."

"That's a heavy commitment," I said. "Janet's sixteen and Mark is what? About fourteen? And you already have two teenage daughters of your own. Teenagers are a challenge in the best of circumstances, and Janet and Mark would bring a few problems with them."

Dean nodded. "We're a close family right now. I don't want to do anything that will hurt my relationship with Sandy and

DeeDee. There are other considerations too. We don't have a lot of room in the house. We don't have a lot of money. I don't know if I can be a good foster father to Janet and Mark. They're good kids and I really like them. It's just that—"

"Yeah. It's a tough adjustment to make."

"I don't know if I'm up to it, Ron." He sighed deeply. "But if I don't help these kids, what'll happen to them?"

"How does Louise feel about it?" I asked.

"We're working on this together with our kids. We all just want to do what God wants us to do."

We fell silent for a while, and I saw tears roll down the cheeks of this rugged carpenter. I was reminded of the tender heart of another rugged Carpenter of two thousand years ago. A tender heart for children, for people who are hurting, for people who are spiritually hungry: I saw the tears of Jesus on the face of my friend.

We prayed together, then just sat there on the dock, looking at the lake, watching the sun go down and the stars come out.

Finally, I said, "What are you thinking, Dean?"

"I think God wants me to take the kids."

"You're sure?"

"No, not sure. But I feel God nudging me in this direction." He stood and offered me his hand. "Let's go home."

That was what our relationship was like. I was Dean's pastor, and he was my mentor. He was nearly twice my age and a man of profound faith and character, yet he didn't hesitate to seek my company, my counsel, my prayers. I learned from him the importance of vulnerability, of having the freedom to cry, of being willing to express fear and weakness at a time of decision.

I also learned something of the mutual nature of a mentoring relationship. Even though I looked up to Dean, even though our relationship centered on Dean's being a friend to me, encouraging me, counseling me, and praying for me, he could still reach out and say, "Ron, this time I need you to be a friend to me." I was the learner, yet our relationship was a two-way street.

After leaving Mt. Ayr and moving first to Minneapolis and then to California, I've carried something of Dean Frost along with me. I've always wanted to have his kind of impact on others and have tried to emulate the openness, vulnerability and compassion I saw in him. Over the past twenty years, as my wife, Shirley, and I have opened our own home to young people, there's a sense in which it was actually Dean swinging the door wide and saying, "You're welcome here." In recent years, I've become more acutely aware of the profound influence this godly man had on my life, and I've come to realize that in emulating the life-style he lived, I'm living the life of a mentor.

THE MAKING OF A MENTOR

I've spent many years in classrooms, absorbing information, ideas, and skills. I'll always be grateful for my formal education. Yet when I look back over all the influences that have shaped my mind, values, faith, and character, I have to conclude that my life has been impacted far more dramatically by a few important people—my mentors—than by the formal educational process.

Many people have invested their lives in mine. And I, in turn, am investing my life in others. In the pages to come, you will meet some of these people, both my mentors and some whom I have mentored. My co-author, Jim Denney, has interviewed some of these special people in my life and has interwoven their experiences and reflections on the mentoring process throughout this book. Through their examples and through the Scriptures, we will explore how God uses mentoring relationships to make us all we're meant to be in Christ.

My dictionary gives this definition of a mentor:

Men′ · tor / *n*. [from *Mentor,* friend of Odysseus] 1. a trusted counselor or guide. 2. a teacher or coach.

This definition illuminates three facets of what it means to be a mentor.

First, we learn that the word *mentor* derives from the name of a character in Homer's *Odyssey*. In this ancient Greek tale, King Odysseus of Ithaca entrusted his only son, Telemachus, to the care and training of his wise friend, Mentor, while he himself went off to war. In the character of Homer's Mentor, we find components of wisdom, caring, and commitment to training the next generation—all essential ingredients for the making of a mentor.

Second, this definition calls a mentor "a trusted counselor or guide." Underscore that word *trusted*. A mentor earns respect and trust by the quality and genuineness of his or her life.

Third, this definition suggests that a mentor is a teacher or coach. In my experience, one specific kind of coach captures a crucial dimension of what it means to be a mentor: a *player-coach*.

A number of years ago when I was Bible teacher for the Minnesota Vikings, I got to see a real player-coach in action: my friend Jeff Siemon. He then played middle linebacker for the Vikings and called signals for every defensive play. Because he was a *player*-coach, Jeff didn't just bark orders from the sidelines. He didn't have to shout "Hustle! Hit harder! Move left! Go downfield! Use your head!" because he was right there on the field, leading by his own example. He demonstrated by his own grit what it means to hustle, to dig in and hit the opposition, to make the right moves, to be mentally agile in the clinches, to be focused on the goal.

Jeff is a player-coach-mentor off the field as well as on. He's a man of deep Christian faith and character, and many people have been attracted to Jesus Christ by the genuineness of his life and testimony. Jeff exemplifies one who stays at your side, not on your back. He gets dirty, sweaty, and bloody just as you do. He inspires your best performance by his own example. To me, that's what being a mentor is all about.

If I were writing my own dictionary, I would define *mentoring* this way:

> **Men′ · tor · ing** / *n*. A process of opening our lives to others, of sharing our lives with others; a process of living for the next generation.

THE STRATEGIC IMPORTANCE OF MENTORS

My friend Mike Flavin knows the power and importance of mentoring relationships. He and I were in a mentoring relationship for several years, both in Minneapolis and in California. Today, Mike is associate pastor to students and families at The Presbyterian Church at New Providence, New Jersey, and he serves on a committee that works with seminary students.

When Mike first began interviewing these young candidates for full-time Christian service, he made a troubling discovery: "None of these people have mentors," he said. "In fact, they have no idea what a mentor *is*. If I say, 'Do you have a mentor?' the answer is usually, 'No.' Of the few that answer, 'Yes,' I probe a little deeper and find out that they are talking about a teacher or an author they admire, but with whom they have little or no personal contact.

"These students are the coming generation of pastors and church leaders, yet they have no models that they are working alongside and learning from in an intensive, practical, hands-on way. They have no one investing in their lives. They have no one taking them under their wing and saying, 'Here's what it's really all about.' All these people are getting is the head knowledge, the theory, the classroom work, the book work. They've never been in the trenches and they don't have the foggiest notion what they're getting into. It's really scary."

MENTORED BY THE BOOKS, MENTORED BY THE MAN

There is a man you've probably heard of who is living the lifestyle of a mentor. He opens his life to others; he shares his life with others; he lives for the next generation. His name is Charles Swindoll.

For years I knew Chuck Swindoll from afar as the pastor of the First Evangelical Free Church of Fullerton, California, and as the author of such books as *The Grace Awakening, Improving Your Serve,* and *Growing Strong in the Seasons of Life.* In fact, Chuck had a profound mentoring influence on me long before I ever met him, because I had read every book he had ever written. In those books and in his radio preaching, I found a man who modeled Christlike grace, a deep commitment to the Scriptures, and an appreciation for joy and laughter.

In recent years, I've come to know Chuck personally, through our mutual commitment to mentoring. Each year Chuck takes the young men of his staff on a tour of West Coast churches, including the church I serve in the Bay area. And I do the same, taking the young men on my staff to several southern California churches, including First Evangelical Free Church in Fullerton. Chuck's goal and mine is to immerse those who work alongside us in a variety of experiences and approaches to Christian service, as practiced in a variety of churches.

Peter Hiett, a friend and an associate pastor of our church, describes this experience from the perspective of someone who is committed to being mentored at the same time he is a mentor to young people: "We call this the 'Under 30 Trip.' Ron takes all the church staff members under age 30 in a van to southern

California. We go to six churches, meet the staff of each
church, ask questions, and get a feel for how things are done in
other settings. Afterward, we sit in the van, talk about what we
liked, what we could implement in our own church, and what
probably wouldn't work. It's a great learning experience, and a
great time of getting to know Ron better."

The Under 30 Trip is one mentoring strategy I've learned
from Chuck Swindoll. He has also taught me a lot about what it
means to demonstrate integrity and courage in the public spotlight. Through his books, his preaching, and the quality of his
life, Chuck continues to be a mentor to me.

You don't need to be an author, a pastor, a professor, or a
super-spiritual guru to be a mentor. You don't need a Ph.D., or
even a college education. Mentoring simply means we are
committed to influencing others by the example of our lives.
Mentoring can and should be a natural part of who we are in
every arena of life: church, business, friendships, and family.

The purpose of mentoring is not merely to impart knowledge
to others (although mentoring has an educational dimension).
The purpose of mentoring is not merely to impart skills to
others (although mentoring has a training dimension as well).
Rather, authentic Christian mentoring deals primarily with issues of maturity and integrity, and only secondarily with information and skills. It has much more to do with modeling
character than with verbal teaching. It has more to do with
what is *caught* than what is *taught*.

My friend Joe Pettit, senior pastor of the First Presbyterian
Church in Sanger, California, makes this analogy about the
mentoring process: "If you take a brick of lead and a brick of
gold and rub them together, then look at them, it seems at first
that nothing has changed. But if you examine the surfaces of
both bricks very closely, in the lead brick you find tiny flecks of
gold, and in the gold brick you find tiny flecks of lead.

"That's what the mentoring process is like: a little of me becomes part of you, and a little of you becomes part of me. Romans 8:29 talks about being conformed to the likeness of Christ. The mentoring process has a lot to do with sharing our Christlikeness with others, so that those best aspects of who we are in Christ can be soaked up by others."

THE MENTORING TRADITION

Mentoring is not a new idea. In fact, mentoring used to be the *only* means of transmitting values, skills, and character qualities from one generation to the next. In past centuries, craftsmen of every calling—from carpenters to metalsmiths to lawyers to the great painters and composers of the Renaissance—employed young apprentices. These apprentices learned not only the skills and craft of their trade, but such intangible dimensions of their calling as pride of craftsmanship, integrity, honesty, diligence, and commitment to excellence.

The mentoring process has produced many, if not most, of the people who have profoundly influenced the ages. Over half of all Nobel prize winners were once apprenticed to other Nobel laureates. From the age of thirteen until his early manhood, the painter and sculptor Michelangelo was mentored by the painter Ghirlandajo. The Russian writer Boris Pasternak, author of *Doctor Zhivago,* was mentored early in life by the novelist Leo Tolstoy and the poet Rainer Maria Rilke. Ludwig van Beethoven spent three years under the mentorship of the Austrian composer Franz Joseph Haydn.

What did Beethoven learn from Haydn? Techniques of composition and counterpoint, certainly. But more importantly, he learned the kind of character one needs to create great music amid tremendous obstacles.

In Haydn, Beethoven found a man who had overcome the childhood pain of repeated physical and psychological abuse from his parents. Beethoven also saw Haydn endure the opposition of a wife who was bitter, quarrelsome, and contemptuous of his music—a wife who often stole Haydn's original manuscripts and used them to line her baking pans! Despite these hardships, Haydn remained cheerful and contented.

In later years, as Beethoven struggled to produce his own art despite his handicap of total deafness, it was not only the technical artistry but the courageous heart and optimistic spirit of his mentor that inspired him to persevere.

In many ways, the history of the highest, most enduring achievements of our culture is also a history of the mentoring process. Only in our own century has mentoring fallen into such disuse—and our society has paid a price for it. In our time, we have witnessed a gradual but steady breakdown of value, of families, of business ethics, of the work ethic, of sexual morality, and of simple civility and human kindness. I'm convinced that much of this social disintegration can be traced to our neglect of the mentoring process.

An old Chinese proverb expresses the long view of history embraced by the mentoring process:

> If you are planting for a year, plant grain.
> If you are planting for a decade, plant trees.
> If you are planting for a century, plant people.

Mentors plant not only for a century, but for millennia—and indeed, for eternity.

Wherever we see lives being changed and Christian values being advanced, we usually find that a biblical mentoring process is at the heart of that transformation. We find strong elements of mentoring in the discipleship training programs of

Dawson Trotman and the Navigators, of John Alexander and InterVarsity Christian Fellowship, of Jay Kesler and Youth for Christ. All these twentieth-century programs trace their roots back to the Master Mentor who called twelve people to himself with the words, "Follow me."

From the life and example of Jesus, we derive the fundamental concept of mentoring:

> More time spent with fewer people equals greater lasting impact for God.

It's a principle as old as the Word of God: "As iron sharpens iron," says the book of Proverbs, "one man sharpens another."[1] Moses mentored Joshua. Naomi mentored her daughter-in-law, Ruth. Ezra mentored Nehemiah. Elijah mentored Elisha. Elizabeth mentored her cousin Mary. Barnabas mentored Paul and John Mark. Paul mentored his spiritual son Timothy. Paul also mentored Priscilla and Aquila, who in turn mentored Apollos.

Jesus transformed the world because he poured his life into the Twelve. Though he preached to the masses, he invested himself in a few, knowing that those few would invest themselves in still others, and thus transform the world. If we want to transform our families, our churches, our businesses, our communities, and ultimately our world, then we must discover what it means to pour our lives into individuals. We must learn to spend more time with the few. We must learn to live for the next generation. We must become mentors.

NO "RIGHT" WAY TO MENTOR

Who should seek to be mentored? Anyone and everyone.
Who should seek to become a mentor to others? Again, any-

one and everyone. All it takes to profoundly influence the lives of others is love and commitment. ☆ ☆ ☆

Ken Heileger has been a lifelong mentor to me. He began investing in my life when I was about nine years old and continues to invest in my life to this day. Ken was my Sunday school teacher in fourth, fifth, and sixth grades. He had some unorthodox teaching methods, such as rewarding his students with a nickel, dime, or quarter for memorizing Scripture. He was a tremendous model of Christian love.

Throughout my junior high and high school years, Ken never missed a sporting event or choir concert in which I or one of his other students participated. And even into my college years, Ken sent me notes and letters with a specially selected verse of Scripture, and often included a check for $5 or $10 to help with my expenses. Ken had such an impact on my life that I asked him to speak in both my ordination and installation services when I served in my first church.

Ken and his wife, Ann, never had children of their own, but in a very real way, they've had hundreds of children. Step into Ann's kitchen, and you see dozens of photos taped onto the walls and the refrigerator—photos of young adults Ken and Ann have mentored. And while others may have diplomas and certificates of special recognition on their office walls, Ken's office is filled with pictures of men and women to whom he has given his time and energy.

Now in his seventies, Ken continues to mentor me. On my most recent trip to the Midwest, Ken drove two hours each evening to hear me give a week-long series of talks, then took me out afterward to talk about our lives and our faith.

Is there such a thing as a "mentor's personality"? Yes, in the sense that literally *anyone* who loves people and wants to make a positive difference in the lives of others has a "mentor's personality." But there is no one "right" mentoring model. What ultimately determines the effectiveness of the mentoring process is not a person's style or skills or temperament, but a person's character, commitment, and love.

The world is full of people who want to impart what they know by writing a book, by teaching a class, by preaching a sermon, by leading a seminar. Those are all good things, and I myself have done and continue to do all those things. But I can't help feeling that while there are many authors, teachers, and preachers in the world, there are sadly too few mentors. For all the thousands who are eager to share their knowledge and skills with others, there are just a handful who are willing to share their *lives*, who are willing to be transparent, vulnerable, and open about their successes and their failures, their joys and their pain, their faith and their doubts.

One dreary day during World War II, in a loathsome place in southern Poland called Auschwitz, a group of Nazi guards discovered that a prisoner was missing from one of the cell blocks. In retaliation for the escape, the guards selected ten men to die an excruciating death in the starvation bunker. One of the condemned, Sergeant Gajowniczek, sobbed, "My poor wife! My poor children!" as the guards stripped him and his companions of their shoes and clothing.

Suddenly, both the guards and the prisoners were startled as an old man stepped forward and addressed the Kommandant. "I would like to die in the place of one of these men," the old man said.

"In whose place do you wish to die?" the Kommandant asked warily.

"Him," the prisoner replied, pointing to Gajowniczek, "the one with the wife and children."

"And who are you, Number 16670?" asked the Kommandant, checking the number on the elderly prisoner's clothing.

"Just a Catholic priest."

The Nazis called priests *die schweinerischen Pfaffen,* or "pig-priests," and considered them the second lowest form of life in the camp, next to Jews. The old man had chosen his words carefully, to give himself the greatest chance of being allowed to die. The Kommandant replied, "Accepted."

The priest, Father Maximilian Kolbe, took his place with the other nine, and Gajowniczek was returned to the cell block. Who was this man who offered his life as a sacrifice for another?

Father Kolbe was a Polish Franciscan priest who, before his arrest in 1941, vocally opposed Nazism, both from his pulpit and over national radio. Sentenced to Auschwitz for aiding Jews and the Polish underground, he lived the life of a mentor among his fellow prisoners. He prayed with and encouraged them, talking daily with them about Jesus. He cheerfully shared his meager rations with his fellow prisoners, and finally gave his life for them. He willingly walked naked into the starvation bunker with nine other condemned men.

A Polish worker named Bruno Borgowiec was sent into the bunker every day to haul the dead to the crematorium. Borgowiec had been in the starvation bunker many times, performing the same grisly task among other doomed men, but this time was different. He later compared the experience to "descending into the crypt of a church."[2] Instead of the usual moans and curses, he heard prayers, hymns, and the recitation of the rosary. He heard not just Father Kolbe's voice, but the voices of all the men, joined in praise to God. One guard looked into the serene face of Father Kolbe, then emerged from the bunker muttering, "The priest is a real man. We never had one of his kind here before."[3]

Borgowiec described how Kolbe mentored his doomed companions even in the last days of their lives. "He asked for nothing and never complained," he said. "He inspired the others with courage, urging them to hope that the fugitive . . . would still be found, and that they would then be set free."[4] Whenever a man seemed on the verge of unconsciousness or death,

Borgowiec recalled, Kolbe would pray with that man and bid him farewell.

The hymns and prayers of the survivors lost strength as the men began their second week in the bunker. One by one, the prisoners died.

At the end of two weeks, four men remained alive. Only Father Kolbe was conscious. Suddenly, the door of the bunker was flung open. Borgowiec entered in the company of SS guards and the camp doctor. In the doctor's hands were four syringes of carbolic acid. The Nazis had decided to end the lives of the last four survivors, not as a kindness but as a simple expediency. The starvation bunker was needed for a new group of victims.

Father Kolbe, now just a living skeleton, sat against the wall, a smile on his lips, his hands in his lap. The doctor injected the three unconscious victims first. Then he went to Kolbe, who muttered a prayer while holding out his arm to receive the injection. Borgowiec looked away. A few moments later, Father Kolbe was dead.

Maximilian Kolbe lived the life of a mentor until the last moment of his human existence. His life was spilled out like water—but it was not wasted. He willingly poured himself into the men who died with him, into the men of the cell block who survived him, into Sergeant Gajowniczek, into Bruno Borgowiec, and even into the SS guards who watched his life and death with amazement.

That is our task in the days that are left to us on this earth: to pour ourselves into the lives of other people. As imitators of the Master Mentor, we seek to live the hours and moments that remain to us for the sake of God and the sake of others. Our goal is to see that what God has built into our lives—our Christlike maturity and refined character—is not merely preserved but *multiplied* in future generations.

THE STRATEGY OF THE MASTER

In its truest form, in the deepest sense, the life of a follower of Christ is the life of a mentor.

This, then, is our aim in the remaining pages of this book: to rediscover—in real, practical ways that apply to our lives in the 1990s—the bold strategy Jesus the Master used to transform the world. I will draw on examples from the Scriptures, from history, from the business world, from my own experience, and from the experience of friends who have shaped my life, and friends whose lives I have helped to shape. At the request of the editors, my co-author, Jim Denney, has interviewed many of these people. In the words of these friends, we will give you their side of the mentoring experience as well as mine. Through these pages, we will explore such questions as:

- How do I select a mentor?
- How do I become a mentor?
- When should I be tender as a mentor? And when should I be tough?
- How can I become a more effective motivator and energizer of other people?
- And much more.

So join me in a life-changing, world-changing adventure. Together, let's place our sandals in the footprints of the Master and learn his timeless strategy for transforming lives.

A strategy called *mentoring*.

Chapter 2

A LEARNER'S NOTEBOOK

How do you select a mentor?

MENTORING AT SUNRISE

Lorne Sanny was a young man in need of a mentor.

He studied the Scriptures and saw the revolutionary difference mentoring relationships made in the lives of the twelve disciples, of Paul, of Timothy, and of so many others. He knew he needed that kind of influence in his own life. So he prayed and asked God to lead him to a mentor. The answer God gave him: Talk to Dawson Trotman, the founder and president of an international discipleship ministry called the Navigators.

Sanny sought out Dawson Trotman and said, "I know how busy you must be, but I was wondering if you could give me just an hour a week? Or maybe even an hour a month? I really need someone to give me some time, to guide me and help me focus my life."

Dawson fixed a piercing gaze on this young man and asked, "Are you really serious about this?"

"Yes, sir."

"Good," said Trotman. "What are you doing at five o'clock tomorrow morning?"

"Well, I—" Sanny paused. What he normally did at that hour of the morning was *sleep*.

"That's the only time I have free," Trotman continued. "I can meet with you at 5:00 A.M., once a week. What do you say?"

Sanny grinned. "I say there's no sense sleeping my life away."

"Amen to that," Trotman said, returning the grin. "I'll see you at the lake. Don't forget your Bible."

The next morning, Sanny arrived at the shore of the lake of Glen Eyrie, the Navigators retreat near Colorado Springs. Trotman was already there, and had built a big fire to ward off the pre-dawn chill.

Week after week, Dawson Trotman kept that 5:00 A.M. appointment with Lorne Sanny. He shared his thoughts and his wisdom with Lorne. He poured his life into him.

Today, Dawson Trotman is dead, but his commitment, discernment, and spirit live on in Lorne Sanny, who is director of business and professional ministries of the Navigators.

What was true for Lorne Sanny is true for you and me. If you want to be all you were meant to be in Christ, you need to have someone in your life who can build you up, guide you, encourage you, challenge you, and expand your vision for what you can become. You need a mentor. A mentoring relationship is worth getting up early for, worth losing sleep over, worth sacrificing for.

HOW TO FIND A MENTOR

So what do you look for in a mentor?

First, select someone you admire. Do you share that person's values and philosophy of life? Do you admire that person's character qualities—courage, faith, integrity, compassion, wisdom, discernment, strength, and love—and do you want to grow to possess those same qualities?

Second, select someone who believes in people, who is committed to relationships, who has a positive outlook. Choose someone who is an encourager rather than a critic. This doesn't mean you don't ever want to be confronted by your mentor. The whole point of a mentoring relationship is to challenge you with new ways of thinking and doing things, so that you can change and grow. But you want to make sure that, whatever difficulties might arise in the relationship, you will have the kind of mentor who seeks to build you up, not tear you down.

Third, choose a person who will genuinely rejoice in your growth and achievements, someone who is interested in you and pulling for you, not someone who will feel threatened by your progress.

How do you find such people? You begin with prayer. Ask God to open your eyes and help you discover a mentor. Potential mentors are all around you, in the very streets and corridors you walk every day. Could it be your employer or your teacher? A pastor, elder, or layperson in your church? Your Bible study leader? Your next-door neighbor?

Sometimes, when you have prayed, you have to patiently wait for God to answer. But be sure you wait with your eyes open. Be ready to recognize that special person God wants to reveal to you—that person who demonstrates Christlike character, a positive approach to life, a commitment to relationships, and availability. You may find your mentor in the place you'd least expect.

A young man named Josh found *his* mentor under his own house!

"Well, Josh," said Mr. Springer, clambering up from the crawlspace beneath the house, "looks like I found your problem. Simple matter to fix. You should get down there and take a look at the plumbing you've got under this old house. A thing of beauty. Copper pipes throughout. They don't build 'em that way anymore."

"You know, Mr. Springer," said Josh, "you're amazing."

"Who, me?" said the plumber, grinning bashfully.

"Yes, you. I mean, this is the third or fourth time I've had you out here to work on our plumbing. You always come with a big smile on your face, you're always whistling and singing, and most of all, you always seem to love your work. It's as if you look at plumbing as an art form. You've been a plumber for—what? Thirty years? Yet you still approach your work as if it were a fascinating challenge."

Mr. Springer laughed. "I do, indeed, young man!" he said. "Don't you? I'd think you'd have the same feel for your own line of work. After all, advertising is a fascinating business."

"I used to think so," said Josh. "But I've been in advertising for five years now and I'm ready to chuck it. I don't even want to go to the office anymore. What's your secret?"

" 'Whatever you do, do it heartily, as to the Lord and not to men,' " said Mr. Springer. "Colossians 3:23. Whenever I fix a pipe or install a shower pan or replace a busted toilet, I'm doing the Lord's work. I'm the Lord's plumber, and he deserves the best I can give him."

In a flash, Josh understood something about the nobility— and even the *holiness*—of labor. He wanted to learn more. Josh and Mr. Springer talked for another twenty minutes. Mr. Springer spoke of the values and principles he had learned from his own father, and which he was seeking to build into his two sons. Josh told Mr. Springer about the father he couldn't remember, because he had died when Josh was only four. By the end of their talk, these two men had agreed to meet for breakfast the following week—an appointment they continued to keep for two years.

Where should you look for your mentor? Where do you go to find a person of wisdom, integrity, and joy who can teach you how to become more mature in Christ? Keep your eyes open to unexpected possibilities. Pray that God will send you a mentor and that you will be sensitive to recognize the person God sends you. Be interested in people. Engage people in conversation about their work, their history, their values. Prepare to be surprised.

After all, Josh found his mentor under the floor of his own house. Where will you find *your* mentor?

MY SEARCH FOR MENTORS

Some of the most influential mentoring relationships in my life were forged during my college and graduate school years. Regardless of the career we choose—ministry, business, public service, media, education, entertainment—the arena of higher education is usually one of the most strategic places in life to form mentoring relationships. The three men who served as invaluable models to me during that formative time in my own life were Addison Leitch, Donald Bloesch, and Bob Guelich.

Addison Leitch was the chaplain and vice president of Tarkio College in Tarkio, Missouri, where I attended my junior and senior years. Even before attending Tarkio, I knew Addison well, for he was a close friend of our family and was often a guest in our home. Addison was also married to Christian author Elisabeth Elliot for a brief time, until his death due to cancer.

The author of *Interpreting Basic Theology,* a book on theology for laypeople, Addison engaged me in many stimulating, challenging discussions during my college years, and he taught me a lot about what it means to apply biblical truth to the rough-and-tumble experiences of everyday life. He often invited me to assist with the Wednesday night chapel services, then he and I would retire to his house to chat about his message or just to talk about life.

My mentor during my masters program in seminary was a brilliant evangelical theologian named Donald Bloesch, the author of many important books on theology, including *The Re-*

form of the Church, Essentials of Evangelical Theology, and *The Struggle of Prayer.*

My mentor and friend during my doctoral work was Bob Guelich. I got to know Bob not only as the supervisor of my doctoral research, but as a fellow member of a group of men who prayed together weekly. Bob, the author of *The Sermon on the Mount* (considered by many the classic commentary on Matthew 5—7 in the twentieth century), taught me what it means to be a diligent *student* of the Word and a faithful *doer* of the Word, as well.

These three men—Addison Leitch, Donald Bloesch, and Bob Guelich—made a crucial investment in my life during my bachelor, masters, and doctoral work. They were people with great minds, with notable accomplishments, with books and degrees to their credit. Yet what stands out so vividly in my mind about these men is the way each invested his time and his caring in my life.

As I moved from school life to professional life, my need for mentoring relationships did not diminish. On the contrary, I've made it a practice to actively seek the company and advice of older, wiser people throughout my career. One such man is Ray Stedman, pastor of the Peninsula Bible Church in Palo Alto, California.

I had known *of* Ray Stedman for years before I met him, having been influenced by his book, *Body Life.* Then, in the mid-1970s, I was introduced to Ray by a mutual friend, Jeff Siemon of the Minnesota Vikings. Ray came to Minneapolis, where I was then living and working, and spent a week ministering in our church and staying in our home. During the many talks we had during that week, Ray challenged me to practice systematic, expositional preaching. And his gracious challenge completely changed my approach to my vocation.

Now that I am on the West Coast, I see Ray frequently, and he has become a spiritual father to me. When a serious challenge arises in my own work, I know I can call Ray at a moment's notice, and he'll be able to put the problem into a realistic, biblical perspective.

There are others like Ray, whom I used to know only by listening to their tapes or reading their books, but now know as friends and mentors. One of these is Leighton Ford.

Some time ago, Leighton and I met for lunch at a restaurant at the San Francisco Airport. Amid a whirlwind tour of evangelistic rallies and leadership training seminars, this friend and mentor took the time to be with me and listen to me. We talked at length about my tendency to schedule every hour of the week so tightly that I leave no time for the "ministry of interruptions"—those unexpected, unplanned needs that arise from time to time in the lives of people around me.

"Ron, my friend," he said, "remember how Jesus would stop in the middle of ministering to hundreds of people, so that he could heal the paralytic man who was let down through the roof, or so that he could heal the woman with a flow of blood. Now, how will you be able to meet those kinds of unscheduled needs in your own work if you are so boxed in, locked in, and walled off by your schedule that you can't break away for five, ten, or twenty minutes?"

I had to confess that Leighton was right. You would expect that Leighton, one of the most sought-after Christian speakers in the world, would schedule his time even more tightly than mine. Yet wherever I go, whenever people mention Leighton Ford, they talk about how available he is, and how sensitive he is to the needs of individuals. That's a Christlike dimension I want to build into my own life.

As I reflect on all the people who have sculpted my life (of whom I had space to mention only a few), I can clearly see the Mentoring Principle in operation: More time spent with fewer people equals greater lasting impact for God. I see it in the lives of my own mentors—busy, successful people involved in important work, writing books, making public appearances, reaching lives by the scores, the hundreds, or even the millions. Yet each of these people has felt a need to be in close mentoring relationships with others, sharing their lives with others, living for the next generation.

What do I carry within me of men like Dean Frost, Addison Leitch, Donald Bloesch, Bob Guelich, Ray Stedman, Leighton Ford, Chuck Swindoll, and all the others who have had a hand in sculpting my life and my character?

Skills, information, knowledge, leadership ability? A deeper understanding of what it takes to do the job of a pastor? Yes, I owe all of these to my mentors. But these are not the *products* of the mentoring process. These are just the by-products.

The one thing I carry away from my mentors which I treasure above all else is what I have learned from them about *how to become more like Jesus*.

Most of what is good within me was put there by my mentors. And all that has been entrusted to me, I want to multiply in the lives of others.

That is why I want to be mentored and why I want to mentor others.

DO WOMEN NEED MENTORS?

Are mentoring relationships as important for women as for men? Absolutely! In these times of shifting and uncertain values, when the role of women in our culture is continually being redefined, women have a special need for supportive, enriching, encouraging relationships. Women in the workplace have special needs—for career advice, for professional contacts, for help with discrimination and pay issues, for time management counseling, for dealing with sexual harassment—that can best be met by mentoring relationships with other women. This is even more true of single mothers, who must juggle the responsibilities of job, home, child-care, often amid the turmoil of bitter relations with an ex-husband.

Another group of women whose needs are frequently ignored these days are stay-at-home mothers, who have the enormous responsibility of mentoring their children while running their homes. Increasingly, it takes two paychecks just to maintain a modest lifestyle, and the women who elect to make motherhood a full-time job frequently have to make enormous sacrifices. These women need the encouragement and guidance of other women who have been there. They need mentors.

Two significant woman-to-woman mentoring relationships are described in the Scriptures. In the Old Testament, Ruth is mentored by her mother-in-law, Naomi. As their story opens in the book of Ruth, these two women have just lost their husbands. It's a time of famine, and they are alone in the world with no one to provide for them. Naomi, a Jew, urges Ruth, a woman of Moab, to leave her, to go back to her people, to marry and make a life for herself. But Ruth clings to Naomi and says,

> Wherever you go, I will go;
> And wherever you lodge, I will lodge;
> Your people shall be my people,
> And your God, my God.[1]

Ruth stays with Naomi and learns from her. They support each other through the time of famine. And when Ruth marries and has a child, Naomi becomes the child's godmother and helps to raise him.

In the New Testament, Mary the mother of Jesus is mentored by her older cousin, Elizabeth. In Luke 1, Mary spends three months in the home of Elizabeth, building a relationship of sharing, trust, and encouragement. Mary, a betrothed teenager, learns from Elizabeth what marriage is supposed to be and how a wife in that culture relates to her husband and cares for her baby.

Paul specifically carved out a mentoring role for mature Christian women when he wrote that they should be "teachers of good things . . . [and should] admonish the young women to love their husbands, to love their children, to be discreet, chaste, homemakers, good, obedient to their own husbands, that the word of God may not be blasphemed."[2]

A LEARNER'S HEART

What should I, as a learner, bring to the mentoring relationship?

A story is told about a Zen teacher named Nan-In, who lived in nineteenth-century Japan. Nan-In was having tea in his garden when a university professor came to visit. "How may I help you?" asked Nan-In.

"I've come to inquire into wisdom," said the professor. "I wish to learn from you."

"Ah," said Nan-In. "Be seated and we shall talk about wisdom. May I serve you tea?"

"Yes, thank you," said the professor, seating himself on the mossy ground across a low table from the Zen teacher.

Nan-In set a cup before the professor and began pouring tea. He talked as he poured, fixing his gaze on the eyes of his visitor. The professor was so intent on what Nan-In was saying, that it was several moments before he glanced down and saw that the teacup was overflowing and Nan-In was *still pouring*. "Stop!" the professor suddenly cried in alarm. "You have overfilled the cup!"

Nan-In smiled and stopped pouring. "Yes, my friend, the cup is overfull. You are like this cup, so full of your own ideas and opinions. How can I teach you any wisdom until you first empty your cup?"

Empty People

The first ingredient a learner must bring to a mentoring relationship is his own emptiness, his own teachability. Just as it is the empty volume within a cup that makes it useful, it is the empty volume within us that enables us as learners to receive from our mentors and to be useful to God.

Emptiness was what the Master Mentor required from his learners. When Nicodemus the Pharisee came to Jesus seeking wisdom, Jesus confronted his fullness of knowledge, telling him he must become like a newborn baby. To the rich young ruler, the Master Mentor said, "Empty yourself of all you have and come, follow me!" But the rich young ruler was too full of his own worldly values to learn from Jesus, and he went away sorrowing.

Who were the learners Jesus gathered around himself? People without education, like the fishermen Simon and Andrew and James and John. People without self-esteem, such as the despised tax collectors, Matthew and Zacchaeus. People broken by sin, such as Mary Magdalene. In short, *empty* people.

I suspect the mentoring process will always be an unpopular process, because it requires us to empty ourselves of our own opinions and expectations. This has been true at least as far back as the time of Christ. At one time the Master Mentor was surrounded by scores of followers. But the more he taught about who he was and what his purposes were in the world, the less popular he became. His followers began to fall away, to desert him, until there were only twelve left—and one of them was a traitor. All he had with which to change the world was eleven underachieving, mostly illiterate men. But they were *teachable*—and that was enough.

To be empty and teachable means that we refuse to let our ego get in the way of our learning and growing. We will be tempted to try to impress our mentor with what we already know, with what we can do. And whenever we do that, we shut off our own ability to receive.

PAGES FROM MY NOTEBOOK

Besides being empty and teachable, what does the learner need to be willing to do?

First, we need to apply what we are learning. The mentoring process is not just about the transfer of information. If it were, you wouldn't need a mentor; you'd just need a book. Whatever we absorb and assimilate from our mentor—whether job skills or faith or leadership ability—we should test and put into practice in the laboratory of life.

Second, we should set up a regular, disciplined schedule in which to meet with our mentor. It's frequently helpful to have some sort of "core" activity around which to build the mentoring relationship—a Bible study, a book study, a project, or a task. Come prepared. Bring questions, ideas, or reflections that come to you as you continue thinking and studying between your regular sessions together. Make your time together count.

Third, be committed to the mentoring relationship. Don't give up. Don't let it slide. Be persistent. Be consistent.

Fourth, respect your mentor—but don't idolize him or her. Every mentor has flaws as well as virtues, and we dare not allow ourselves to be blinded to those flaws.

The goal of mentoring is not just to make us more like our mentors, but ultimately to make us more like Christ. So we should take a good, hard look at our mentors and learn from whatever Christlikeness we find, but discard whatever does not resemble the Master Mentor.

Fifth, be accountable. Accountability is the key to maturity and character growth in the Christian life. In *Dropping Your Guard*, Chuck Swindoll defines accountability as:

- Being willing to explain one's actions.
- Being open, unguarded, and nondefensive about one's motives.

- Answering for one's life.
- Supplying the reasons why.[3]

To be accountable means to live your life like an open book before your mentor. You give your mentor permission to ask you personal, probing questions about your private life, your decisions, your motives, your plans, your goals, your beliefs, your hurts, your joys—all because you *trust* your mentor to be looking out for one thing only: your growth and maturity in Christ. You trust your mentor to keep your confidences, to listen to you without judging you, to love you unconditionally, and if necessary to confront you in order to help you to become the person God wants you to be and the person you yourself want to be. To be accountable is to live by the truth of Proverbs 27:6, which says, "Faithful are the wounds of a friend."

Like Chuck Swindoll, Bruce Larson has been an important mentor to me, not only through his books, but through his friendship. I've often trusted him for counsel and encouragement during difficult times in my life. In his book *There's a Lot More to Health Than Not Being Sick,* Bruce says this about accountability:

> Behavioral sciences in recent years have expounded the simple truth that "behavior that is observed changes." . . . Studies done in factories have proven that both quality and quantity of work increase when the employees know that they are being observed. If only God knows what I am doing, since I know He won't tell, I tend to make all kinds of excuses for myself. But if I must report to another or a group of others, I begin to monitor my behavior. If someone is keeping an eye on me, my behavior improves.[4]

This is the foundational principle: *Behavior that is observed changes.* And the necessity of being observed grows greater, not less, as we grow older and assume greater responsibility. To this day, I always make sure that I am involved in a network of mutually accountable relationships. I need to have someone observing my behavior, checking on my progress, helping me meet my personal and spiritual goals, spurring me on to do my best for Jesus Christ.

To this day, I not only mentor others but am mentored by others. I continue to grow, to learn, to mature in Christ. I hope and pray the day never comes when I would say to myself, "I have arrived. I have no more need of mentors. I have no need of other people observing my behavior and holding me accountable." The day I entertain such thoughts is the day I have become arrogant, prideful, and a threat to my own spiritual well-being.

These, then, are a few pages from the notebook of someone who still considers himself as much a learner as a mentor. I still seek the counsel of people who are wiser, more experienced, more battle-scarred than I am. I'm sure I always will. My notebook is far from full. I still have much to learn.

Yet I have also learned much. I want to pass the things I've learned along to the next generation.

But that's another chapter.

Chapter 3

BECOMING A MENTOR

Be what you would have your pupil be

THE MARK OF A TRUE MENTOR

Today, there are very few people who have read the books of Sherwood Anderson, or who even know his name. But for a time during the early twentieth century, his fiction works such as *Dark Laughter* and *Winesburg, Ohio* made Anderson one of the most popular writers in America. And during those years, Anderson mentored dozens of young, aspiring novelists.

One of Anderson's protégés was a young man who had been wounded as an ambulance driver in World War I. Shortly after his release from the army, this young man rented an apartment near Anderson's on the Near North Side of Chicago. He spent a year talking with Anderson, sharing meals with him, writing and showing his stories to Anderson—stories which his mentor critiqued with brutal frankness. Six years later, while still in his twenties, this young man published a novel called *The Sun Also Rises*. Immediately, he became an international sensation. His name was Ernest Hemingway.

Another man who was mentored by Anderson had written only a few poems and amateur stories when he first met Anderson in 1925. By that time, Sherwood had moved to New Orleans and was the leading figure in a circle of Southern writers. Hungry to learn the craft, the commitment, and the character one needs to be a successful writer, this young man was inseparable from Anderson for months after their first meeting. During his association with Anderson, this young man produced a novel called *Soldier's Pay,* which Anderson enthusiastically recommended to his own publisher. This novel was the first of a long series of memorable books from the pen of William Faulkner.

The list of people Anderson mentored reads like a *Who's Who* of early twentieth-century American literature, and includes names like John Steinbeck, William Saroyan, and Thomas Wolfe. It was Wolfe who said, "Sherwood Anderson is the only man in America who ever taught me anything." Literary historian Malcolm Cowley called Anderson "a writer's writer, the only storyteller of his generation who left his mark on the style and vision of the generation that followed." He achieved this distinction more by his mentoring of other writers than by his own writing.

The mark of a true mentor is that he rejoices when his pupil surpasses his own achievements. That's what the poet Walt Whitman meant when he wrote,

> I am the teacher of athletes,
> He that by me spreads a wider breast
>   than my own proves the width of
>   my own.

Or, as Fred Smith, author of *You and Your Network,* put it, "A mentor is not a person who can do the work better than his followers. He is a person who can get his followers to do the work better than he can." I want to live the kind of life Walt

Whitman and Fred Smith described. I want to live my life to inspire and encourage others to do more and greater things than I can do.

WHAT AM I LIVING FOR?

Though the desire to live the life-style of a mentor has been part of me for many years, it has gained strength and urgency in my own mind as I have entered my forties. My brother, who was also my best friend, was in his forties when he passed from this life into eternity. So I'm acutely aware of the brevity of this life, the value of each moment, and the necessity of spending each day as wisely and effectively as possible.

None of us knows how many more breaths we will take, how many more heartbeats we have. We only know they are numbered, and the number is finite. Having reached that time of life when I must realistically address my mortality, I have to ask myself, *What am I living for? What am I leaving behind of myself? What am I investing in?*

Listening to the conversations of my peers, I hear a lot of talk about investing in things like IRAs, 401k plans, stocks, bonds, funds, real estate. And there's nothing wrong with such investments. But as I survey this particular plateau of my life, I feel a need to make a very different kind of investment. I feel an urgency to invest in *people,* to transmit to another generation the faith and heritage that my mentors have so generously invested in me.

There's a saying, "You never see a hearse pulling a U-Haul." A paraphrase of that saying is, "You can't take it with you." The only things of value you and I can take out of this life are the things we did for others and for Jesus Christ. If we want to transform our world, we will begin to invest our lives in others. We will become mentors.

THE LEARNER BECOMES A MENTOR

In the book of Acts, we see a beautiful picture of the transition from learner to mentor in the story of a mentor named Barnabas and his pupil Paul. The writer of Acts first refers to this dynamic duo as "Barnabas and Saul [Paul]": Barnabas the mentor comes first; Paul the learner comes second. In Acts 11, the order remains the same: Barnabas and Paul go to Antioch; Barnabas and Paul minister. But when you get to Acts 13, a significant reversal takes place. The writer no longer refers to "Barnabas and Paul" but "Paul and Barnabas." The pupil has come into his own.

What happened? Did Paul shove Barnabas out of the limelight? No, Barnabas, the Son of Encouragement, wanted it this way. He said, in effect, "I believe in you, Paul. I want to help you, and in this transition time I want to decrease so that you and the gifts God has given you may increase."

This is a beautiful model of biblical mentoring, a model I have always tried to keep before me in my own mentoring relationships. The process goes like this:

Step 1: "I minister, you watch."
Step 2: "We minister together."
Step 3: "You minister, and I watch."
Step 4: "You find another to minister with and to mentor."

This fourth and final step of the Barnabas-Paul mentoring relationship took place when Paul took a young man named Timothy under his wing and began teaching him the ropes of Christian servanthood. Here you see God's multiplication process at work. Barnabas mentored Paul, who, in turn, mentored Timothy (and scores of others); Timothy, in turn, mentored his elders and other Christian servants in his church, and they, in turn, mentored others. Paul stated the principle succinctly in 2 Timothy 2:2: "And the things that you [Timothy] have heard from me among many witnesses, commit these to faithful men who will be able to teach others also."

So, in light of the mentoring relationship of Barnabas and Paul, the questions that confront us are these:

First, do you have a Barnabas in your life? Do you have an encourager? Do you have someone to believe in you, support you, and guide you?

Second, do you have a Paul in your life? Do you have a spiritual mentor who is pouring his life into you the way Paul poured his life into Timothy? Do you have someone you can go to for wise counsel? Someone who serves as an example and a model? Someone who lives out biblical values and spiritual maturity?

Third, do you have a Timothy in your life? Do you have someone in whom to invest your own life? Certainly, you should look upon your spouse and your children as "Timothys," but is there anyone outside your family in whom you are investing yourself?

Every Christian needs a Barnabas, a Paul, and a Timothy in his or her life. There are two ways that you and I live on eternally after our physical death. One way is in heaven, as we live eternally with Jesus Christ. The other way is in the lives of those in whom we have invested ourselves. When we have gone to be with the Lord, will there be young men and women carrying on the biblical truths, the spiritual maturity, the qualities of love and faithfulness and compassion with which we have lived our lives?

"YOU DON'T HAVE TO TAKE A BACK SEAT"

One of the people who has exemplified this Barnabas-Paul-Timothy dynamic in my life is a sparkling Christian young

woman named Barb Cummelin. I've known Barb since she
was in junior high and I was her youth pastor. Today, Barb lives
the life-style of a mentor, getting in the trenches with the young
people she works with as a director of leadership development
and campus life at Seattle Pacific University. She is a
Barnabas-like encourager and a Paul-like mentor to the scores
of "Timothys" in her wide sphere of influence.

Not long ago, Barb reflected on our friendship. "Ron has
been a mentor to me since my teenage years, and he was
always available as a friend," she said. "We'd go out to Burger
King for a Coke, or Ron and Shirley would have me over for
dinner. He let me hang out at his office and we often talked
about life issues, faith, relationships, and growing up.

"Ron was my encourager. He was always offering me leadership opportunities and saying, 'I know you can do this.'
Once, when I was in the ninth grade, he said, 'Barb, I want you
to do the invocation for the Christmas Eve service.' I said,
'Me?! But there'll be 500 people out there!' But he just said, 'I
know you can do it.' And he was right. It was a real confidence
builder for me."

During her high school years, Barb and I often talked together about her future and her goals. She deeply desired a
career in ordained ministry, so we often talked about the issue
of women in the church and whether a career as a pastor was a
realistic and biblical goal for a woman.

"I remember sitting with Ron at the drugstore counter,"
Barb recalls today. "We were sipping Cokes and comparing
Scripture with Scripture on the subject of women in the
church. We looked at both sides of the issue together, and he
always gave me the freedom to make up my own mind about
what the Scriptures said. He believed in me, in my own ability
to search the Scriptures, in my ability to follow the Spirit's
leading and chart my own course in life—and that made *me*
believe in myself."

Barb later graduated from Whitworth College with a Bachelor of Religion degree. At about that time, I took a position as senior pastor of a church in California, and I invited Barb to come out for a summer and take part in a leadership training program there. At the beginning of that summer, Barb was still seeking a career as a pastor. But by the summer's end, all of that had changed.

"It was a really hard time," Barb said. "There was a lot of conflict in that church, and I experienced a lot of exhaustion in the training program due to politics within the church. The summer's experience disillusioned me for a long time afterward. I was turned off by the political structure of the church and seriously questioned if I would ever want to work full-time in a church. I spent a long time processing that experience.

"Even though my summer experience in California was negative, Ron talked it through with me. He helped me to find the positives in it. One of the positives in that experience was that God used it to veer me in another career direction that was complementary but different from what I had planned. Instead of going into the pastoral ministry, I completed grad school and then took a position in the student life area of a Christian college.

"Not long ago, Ron said to me, 'Barb, you're doing everything you wanted to do. You're working with college students in a fulltime ministry. You're using your leadership gifts. You're mentoring young people in your church. You're doing everything you ever wanted to do, but without the title of pastor. This is really everything you dreamed of, only packaged differently.'

"And he was right. It all goes back to those days when Ron and I sat at the drugstore counter, having Cokes, while he said to me, 'Barb, you don't have to take a back seat in life because you're a woman.' It goes back to the way he encouraged me to be open to new things."

Barb Cummelin was one of my Timothys and she continues to be my friend. In her life, I have seen the value and validity of that step-by-step mentoring process: First, "I minister, you watch." And then, "We minister together." Then, "You minister, and I watch." And finally, "You find another to minister with and to mentor."

That's the natural progression of a mentoring relationship.

"YOU CAN'T BEAT FUN!"

Up to now, I suppose I have made mentoring sound like very serious business. And it is. But mentoring should also be fun. In fact, some of the most strategic moments in the mentoring process occur in unplanned, unscheduled, fun times shared between the mentor and the learner.

"I've been in places where the Christian life and Christian ministry are treated as deadly serious business," says my friend and colleague Peter Hiett. "But in this church, there's a great sense of fun and humor on the staff. People don't take themselves too seriously. Ron sets a loose, friendly tone to our work and learning environment, and that makes for bonded, warm relationships on the staff. Relationships are built in both the hard times and the good times, but Ron always makes sure there are a lot of good times to go around."

Joe Pettit, who was my associate during a previous pastorate in California, recalls how much of our mentoring relationship was built on the racquetball court and on the beach. "About once a month," he said, "we took a couple of hours off on a Wednesday afternoon to play racquetball. Because of Wednesday evening services, we were at church from 8:00 A.M. to 9:00 P.M., so we welcomed the afternoon break on the court. And believe it or not, racquetball was a key element in our mentoring relationship. We had so many great conversations in that relaxed, nonprogrammed atmosphere. After we poured ourselves out physically on the court, it seemed easier to talk about real issues. Ron always made sure that the staff had plenty of positive experiences to share together.

"One time, Ron invited Mike Flavin and me to go to the coast for a couple of days. We stayed in a little house not far from the beach, and we spent a lot of time together without any agenda, just talking together about the things that were important to us. We evaluated the past year and laid plans for the future. Mike had accepted a call to another church, so we were saying good-bye as well. We just had a lot of fun and prayed together on the beach. It was a time I'll always remember, because it came straight out of Ron's heart.

"My mentoring relationship with Ron was centered much more on getting close to him as a friend than in merely working together. The sense I always got from Ron is, *I'm interested in you as a person, not just in your usefulness to the program.*

"I try to carry this sense of fun into my own mentoring relationships. I spend time with the guys on my staff, with no other agenda than that of being with their families or simply having fun together. One young man on my staff named Ken is a World War II history buff, like I am. So when we get together for a backyard barbecue, we talk not only about theology and how things are going at church but about the relative merits of the P-51 Mustang and the Supermarine Spitfire.

"Mentoring seems to work best when there is little formal agenda. It's a 'serendipity' kind of thing where, in the Holy Spirit, we say to each other, 'Let's share our lives together. Let's learn from each other. Let's enjoy the pleasure of each other's company.' I think *fun* is an important—but often overlooked—way we help each other become more like Christ."

My friend Barb Cummelin sums up the issue of *fun* this way: "I've learned a lot from Ron about having fun. I know that doesn't sound too spiritual, but I think it's important. Ron just loves life, and that love of life is contagious. When I was growing up, he had this philosophy: *You Can't Beat Fun!* I was lucky to be influenced by someone who is so upbeat and positive."

To this day, a plaque hangs on the wall of my office which reads, "You Can't Beat Fun!" A mentoring relationship is serious and important, but not so serious and important that it shouldn't be *fun!*

THE JOB DESCRIPTION OF A MENTOR

The calling of a mentor is high and noble. The role of a mentor is crucial. The life of a mentor is risky. The rewards of a mentor's work are profound, but intangible. The job description of a mentor is demanding.

If you think you want to be a mentor, then I invite you to consider the following statements which describe the character and attitude a mentor must have and the demands a mentor must meet. Check the statements that apply to you:

1. _____ I am willing to spend the time it takes to build an intensely bonded relationship with the learner.
2. _____ I commit myself to believing in the potential and future of the learner; to telling the learner what kind of exciting future I see ahead for him or her; to visualizing and verbalizing the possibilities for his or her life.
3. _____ I am willing to be vulnerable and transparent before the learner, willing to share not only my strengths and successes, but also my weaknesses, failures, brokenness, and sins.
4. _____ I am willing to be honest yet affirming in confronting the learner's errors, faults, and areas of immaturity.
5. _____ I am committed to standing by the learner through trials—even trials that are self-inflicted as a result of ignorance or error.

6. ____ I am committed to helping the learner set goals for his or her spiritual life, career, or ministry, and to helping the learner dream his or her dream.

7. ____ I am willing to objectively evaluate the learner's progress toward his or her goal.

8. ____ Above all, I am committed to faithfully living out everything I teach.

How many of these eight statements can you honestly, wholeheartedly agree to? This, in fact, is the test of a mentor's heart. And this test is not graded on a curve. It is strictly pass or fail. To follow the mentoring strategy of the Master, we must conform our hearts and wills to his. In these eight statements, you find eight key ingredients of the mentoring strategy, as he practiced it with his own learners, especially with such key learners as Peter and John.

Jesus spent a great amount of time with his disciples. He visualized and verbalized their future. He confronted their sins and errors; he honestly evaluated their progress; yet he unconditionally stood by them and affirmed them and encouraged them. He invited them to be close to him when he was vulnerable, when his heart was breaking in the last few hours before the cross. Most of all, he lived what he taught. Everything he wanted his learners to be, *he was*.

Scottish essayist Thomas Carlyle once wrote, "Be what you would have your pupils be." As mentors, you and I must always keep before us the goal of mentoring: We are not seeking merely to teach the learner, but to *grow* him or her. And growth takes place not merely by hearing, but by *experiencing*. The mentoring process requires that same quality of experiential intensity that the apostle John described when he wrote, "That which was from the beginning, which we have heard, which we have seen with our eyes, which we have looked upon, and our hands have handled, concerning the Word of life."[1]

In truth, the deepest dimensions of the Christian life cannot simply be taught in a classroom or a book. They must be heard, seen, studied intently, handled, lived, and experienced in order to be proven and assimilated.

THE MENTORING OF THE MASTER

When Jesus taught the Twelve about servanthood, not only did he teach them verbally, but he washed their feet. When he taught the Twelve about prayer, not only did he teach them what to pray, he took them out into the garden and prayed with them. Whatever Jesus wanted to teach the Twelve, he taught them not only with his words but by *immersing* them in the experience of his own life.

What Jesus, the Master Mentor, taught you and me by his life is the fact that the Christian life is not just about doctrines and dogmas. It's about character—*Christlike* character. The goal of the Christian life is stated in Romans 8:29: conformity to the image and likeness and character of Jesus Christ. That's why, when Jesus called the Twelve, he didn't say, "Listen to me." He said, *"Follow me."*

Some people think that the purpose of mentoring is to produce the next generation of leaders. And it is true that an effective mentoring relationship will bring out any leadership potential in the learner. But an effective mentoring relationship should enhance any and all ministry potential within the learner, be it leadership, service, encouraging, teaching, giving, mercy, helping, faith, discernment, administration, evangelism, or intercession. It's a tragic mistake to single out leadership as the be-all and end-all of a mentoring relationship.

Dr. Richard Halverson, chaplain of the United States Senate, made a similar observation when he said, "The Church does not need more 'leadership training.' What we need is 'righteousness training.'"[2] Likewise, Becky Pippert, author of

Out of the Saltshaker and Into the World: "We have vastly over-emphasized leadership skills at the expense of character."[3] And Dr. V. Raymond Edman, former president of Wheaton College: "Our job is not to train leaders, but to train servants."[4]

The one act of Christ which more than any other defined and epitomized his mentorship was his act of washing the feet of the Twelve. It was not what most of us would consider an act of leadership. But whenever Jesus demonstrated leadership, he did so by standing our earthly concept of leadership on its head. Jesus led by serving. "I have given you an example," he said to the Twelve after he had washed their feet, "that you should do as I have done to you."[5]

Biblical mentoring is often as much about followership as leadership. The Christian church desperately needs people who can follow, who can serve, who can encourage others, who can teach others, who can sacrificially give, who can evangelize. The church needs people who can work under executive leadership in order to administrate and carry out plans and programs. The church needs people who can help and support and augment the work of the leadership. The church needs people who can pray.

Some prospective mentors may tend to be very selective about who they will mentor, seeking out people who are charismatic, dynamic, handsome—people typically considered "leadership material." This directly opposes the teaching of Scripture and the mentoring model of Jesus, who numbered among his disciples some of the "rejects" and "outcasts" of society. He took this very diverse (and largely "underachieving") group of men and molded them into a force that would change the world.

If Jesus included the "rejects," the "outcasts," and the "underachievers" in his mentoring strategy, shouldn't that be our strategy too? I've tried to make that my own strategy—and sometimes I've succeeded.

Todd Treimer recalls our days together when I was a youth pastor. "Ron taught me to reach out to the 'unlovely' people. There were times I spent the night at his place and the doorbell would ring at three o'clock in the morning. He'd open the door and very graciously take in some teenager who had been kicked out of the house because of a problem involving drugs, pregnancy, or homosexuality. Ron was always willing to spend time with people, lose sleep over people—even people who seemed like losers and outcasts—in order to demonstrate the love of Christ. He never turned off the love, even when it was a real nuisance to love."

Jesus didn't categorize the people to whom he ministered as good people and bad people, as leaders and losers. He saw people not for what they were, but for what they could become. And so should we.

If we only mentor leaders, where will the next generation of followers, helpers, and implementers come from? Our mission as mentors is to train learners not only in the art of leadership, but in the art of followership.

WHAT'S YOUR MOTIVE?

One of the hardest and most important lessons for a mentor to learn is that a mentor is not a master. A mentor is a slave. He is a servant to the learner. He sacrifices his time for the learner. He sacrifices his comfort and privacy for the learner. He washes the feet of the learner.

I would encourage you, before you begin to mentor another person, to carefully, honestly search your motives. Are you attracted to the idea of being a guide or a guru to another person? Does the idea of exercising authority appeal to your pride? Does it boost your self-esteem to see yourself as a sage or a pundit, dispensing your accumulated wisdom to the next generation? If there is a trace of such motivation in you (and be careful! Our motivations have a habit of evading our conscious awareness), then you should deal with those motives before mentoring another person.

Remember that every mentor must also be a learner. Mentoring is mutual. Even as a mentor, be ready to learn from those who are learning from you.

Henry Chin, who was an elder on the church board at one of my previous pastorates, recalls an incident in our relationship that illustrates the mutuality of the mentoring process. "One time," he says, "my phone rang and it was Ron. He wanted to meet with me and get my counsel on a matter. I was so surprised! The man *I* always looked to for counsel wanted *my* advice!

"So we had lunch together and he told me about a situation he was struggling with involving a guest speaker. I always look back on that as a lesson that mentoring is a two-way street."

Another close friend, Ed Aaron, observes, "I look up to Ron as my pastor, my mentor, as a man who teaches me what a man of God should be like. Yet I continually discover what a mutual relationship we have. There have been many times when I have been hurting, and he's been right there beside me. Then there are times when he hurts, and he lets me walk through his struggles with him. If I feel a need to say a word of caring criticism of something he's done, he doesn't take offense. He takes it to heart. Sure, he's the teacher, but he's also teachable."

Every follower of Christ is called to be both a mentor and a learner. Teachers can learn from students. Pastors, elders, and deacons can learn from laypeople. Employers can learn from employees. Leaders can learn from followers. Parents can learn from children. But a mentor who is on a one-way street has very little to give or teach anyone else.

I've known a number of people who wanted to be mentors. Many of them, I'm convinced, craved the ego-gratification of having someone else learn from them, idolize them, emulate them. They craved the recognition of others. They longed to

hear someone say, "Isn't he a wonderful Christian? He's had
an effect on so many lives."

Too many of us want a Christian reputation. Too few of us
want *Christ*. We want to be teachers and masters of others,
when we ourselves are filled with folly and secret addictions to
sin. As Jesus said, we must first remove the log from our own
eye before we are qualified to teach others about the specks in
their eyes.

One of the subtle temptations we face as mentors is the
temptation to seek to reproduce *ourselves* in the next generation rather than to reproduce Christ. A biblical mentor resists
the lure of pride and self-importance that will lead him to clone
himself in his learners.

Our job is to train, guide, encourage, and exhort the learner
according to his or her own gifts and uniqueness, not to make
carbon copies of ourselves. Amos Bronson Alcott, the
nineteenth-century reformer, abolitionist, and educator, observed, "The true mentor defends his pupil against his own
personal influence. He inspires self-trust. He guides their eyes
from himself to the spirit that quickens him. He will have no
disciples." Every mentor should heed Alcott's warning, for the
human heart is easily seduced by something as innocent as the
admiration and eager gratitude of a learner.

In his farewell speech to the elders of the church at Ephesus
in Acts 20, Paul warns about people who would rise within
their own churches and attempt to gather disciples around
themselves. Verses 9 and 10 of 3 John describe one such person, a toxic personality by the name of Diotrephes, "who loves
to have the preeminence" among the people of his church.
Such people are still with us in the church today; don't you be
one of them. A person who mentors others out of a desire to
make disciples or a reputation for himself is a spiritual menace
to his learners, to his church, and to his own soul.

Our goal as mentors must never be to increase ourselves—our reputation, our pride, our self-esteem—but to increase others and exalt Christ. When we focus on encouraging our learners to become *more* of the best they already are rather than focusing on dispensing our own wisdom, achievement, and expertise, then we will become all we were meant to be as mentors. Short of that, all our so-called mentoring amounts to little more than feeding our own egos.

THE ROLE CALL OF ANONYMOUS MENTORS

There's no room for ego-feeding in the mentoring process. Jesus modeled for us the fact that biblical mentoring is a thankless, unattractive, unpretentious calling. I'm convinced that those who have done the most to advance the kingdom of God are the anonymous servants, the unknown mentors who toil in obscurity, neither seeking nor receiving recognition for their labor and dedication. As evidence, I submit the following short quiz (which I've adapted from *Growing Strong in the Seasons of Life* by Charles Swindoll):

1. Who was the elderly woman who believed in Billy Graham and prayed for his salvation every night for ten years?
2. Who built a relationship with a young shoe salesman named Dwight L. Moody? Who led Moody to Christ in his own shoe store and then encouraged him to share his newfound faith with others, setting him on the road to become one of the most effective evangelists of the nineteenth century?
3. Who mentored a young Catholic monk named Martin Luther, helping him to discover the transforming message of grace and freedom at the heart of the New Testament?
4. Who encouraged the English preacher Charles Haddon Spurgeon to persevere through a time of intense criticism and slander regarding his ministry?

5. Who saw and affirmed in a young man named Charles Wesley the ability to write great hymns of praise, long before Wesley himself considered writing music?

How did you score on that quiz? Zero? So did I. The fact is, *each* of these mentors is truly anonymous. And that's the reward of most mentors: obscurity, anonymity, invisibility . . . and one more thing, the words, "Well done, good and faithful servant," spoken in eternity by the Master Mentor himself.

One of the Master's obscure servants was a woman named Dorothea Clapp. Mrs. Clapp used to pray everyday for the students of the high school in her hometown of Ramsey, New Jersey. For decades, she distributed Bible tracts in the train station, taught Sunday school and youth club in a poor community, taught Bible club in her own home, and led Bible memorization classes in which her students learned as many as 300 verses a year. After her own children were grown and had left home, she gave half of her annual income to the support of missionaries.

In the early 1950s, Dorothea Clapp took a special interest in a young Ramsey High School student named George Verwer. She prayed daily for George, and talked to him when she encountered him walking on the sidewalk or in the train station where she passed out tracts. She gave him a Gospel of John and coaxed him into going with her to a Billy Graham meeting. There she prayed with him and led him to the Lord.

From that day on, George was on fire for God. He founded an organization called Send the Light (the name was later changed to Operation Mobilization). Verwer planned to spread Bibles and Christian books in hard-to-reach countries (he was once arrested and deported by the Soviet Union for attempting to distribute Bibles there). Today, Operation Mobilization has hundreds of workers spreading the gospel of Jesus Christ into some of the most hardened and impenetrable countries and cultures in the world, including communist, Moslem, and Hindu nations. The organization also operates two ships which circle the globe, taking Christian literature into ports ranging from Valparaiso to Mombasa, from Karachi to Bombay, from Rangoon to Singapore.

In November 1989, at the age of 88, Dorothea Clapp passed from this life into eternity. But the investment she made in the life of a young Ramsey High School student continues to multiply, compound, and expand in the lives of others throughout the world. A single life she touched so many years ago touches the lives of thousands today.

That's the noblest reward any follower of Christ could hope to see. That's the legacy of a mentor.

PART TWO

THE
ATTRIBUTES
OF A MENTOR

Chapter 4

TENDER TOUGHNESS

Building with steel and velvet

SPEAKING THE TRUTH IN LOVE

Greg eagerly passed the photocopied pages around the conference room table, then sat down. The other staff members picked up their sheets and began glancing through them. I scanned my copy. I noticed a problem with the second paragraph, but the rest of Greg's proposal looked good—excellent, in fact. He had included a lot of creative ideas. I caught Greg's eye and nodded slightly, a nonverbal "Good job!"

"Well, I see one problem right off the bat," said a voice across the table. All eyes turned toward Larry, a staff member, as he added, "Greg, the board will never agree to this stuff in paragraph two!"

I looked back at Greg. His face sagged in disappointment. The meeting continued. The staff discussed Greg's plan and finally accepted it, with changes to the second paragraph. Then we went on to other matters.

After the staff meeting, I walked Larry back to his office. "You know, Larry," I said, closing the door behind us, "your instincts are on target. The board never would have accepted the ideas in that one paragraph. But it would have been better for Greg if we had affirmed the two or three positive things in his plan before jumping on that one problem area. You immediately critiqued the proposal without finding anything to affirm."

"I only said that—" Larry caught himself, then nodded sheepishly. "You're right, Ron."

"You can offer criticism in a way that's gracious and affirming, without compromising the truth. Greg's young and creative. He's got a lot of ideas. In a few years, he'll have a better sense of how those ideas need to mesh with the larger institution. In the meantime, I don't want him to feel he's been shot down."

"I know what you mean, Ron," Larry said. "'Speaking the truth in love,' right? I'll work on it. Oh, and thanks for making me aware of it, brother."

Brother. I liked the sound of that. I was grateful to have a teachable, sincere man of God like Larry on my staff.

It was not a large matter, perhaps, but it's never easy to confront another Christian. And, as head of staff, I am a mentor to every other staff member, including both Larry and Greg. Sometimes, a mentor is called upon to confront. That's when a mentor has to be both tender and tough.

As a mentor, I have earned the credibility to critique Larry's behavior. Larry is one of the most valuable, capable, Christ-centered men I've ever worked with—and I've told him so many times, in many different ways. Because Larry knows I not only appreciate him but continually affirm him, I have the right to be honest and objective with him when it's time to be tough.

As a mentor, I seek to encourage, motivate, and affirm those who are watching me and learning from my life.

ARE YOU AN EVALUATOR OR AN AFFIRMER?

In her book *Balcony People,* Joyce Landorf suggests there are two kinds of people in the world: *evaluators* and *affirmers*. Evaluators are those who tend to look only at performance, who are critical of the faults and mistakes of others, who seek to influence others by judging and correcting them. We can all think of people who have been evaluators in our lives—perhaps a parent, a teacher, a coach, an employer, a pastor, a spouse. Evaluators tend to break the spirit within us, because the first word they usually say to us is a word of criticism.

Then there are the affirmers. Landorf describes affirmers as those whose first word to us is a word of unconditional acceptance and affirmation. Affirmers are much more apt to encourage us to do better next time than to tell us how miserably we failed this time. Affirmers tend to focus more on what we can become than on what we were in the past. Affirmers have the ability to discover qualities and envision potential in us that we never knew we had.

Ed Aaron relates a time in our mentoring relationship when he received some much-needed affirmation. "Ron encouraged me to strike out and make a new start in my life. He saw potential in me that I didn't see in myself. So, with Ron urging me on, I pulled up stakes, moved from Fresno to the Bay Area, and embarked on a brand new life.

"The first few weeks were really rocky. I had a job lined up when I moved, but the first day I reported for work, my employer discovered he had misread my resume. The job evaporated just like that, and I was back on the street, looking for work. I had just moved in with Ron and Shirley, and I was only planning to stay long enough to get my own apartment. I ended up staying with them for three weeks.

"The day I finally landed a job, I called the Davis's and told them the news. When I arrived at the house for dinner that evening, Shirley had already set the table, and she had put in my place a special plate they reserve for people with birthdays, special achievements, and the like. It's a bright red plate that says, 'You Are Special.' I'll tell you, I really felt valued and affirmed that day."

If we want to be effective mentors, we will learn to be affirmers. We will seek to envision and encourage the possibilities that are latent in the learner's character. We will unconditionally accept the learner, even when he fails, and we will encourage him to keep persevering until he reaches his goal.

In her book, Joyce Landorf describes this scenario: You are the parent of a grade school child, and your child brings home a report card. On that report card are five very good grades and one D. What is the first comment you make about that report card? Do you look at those five good grades first and say, "Hey, look at those grades! Good job! I'm sure proud of the work you did in those subjects!" And then do you come back later and add, "Now, let's put our heads together and figure out a way to bring up this grade over here." If that is your response, then you are an affirmer.

But if your response to that report card is to zip right past those five good grades and home in on that one low grade, if your first response is to growl, "What in the world is wrong with you?" then you must admit that you have the tendencies of an evaluator.

Grant, a pastor friend of mine, is living proof that being an evaluator is not an incurable condition. The first time I met him, I immediately found Grant unlikeable, abrasive, and opinionated. But later I learned that Grant came from a broken home, the son of a harsh, critical father who never gave him any affirmation. Growing up, Grant wrapped himself in a protective cerebral shell. He covered up his emotions by projecting a cool, analytical exterior.

One day, he sat down in my office, a worried look on his face. "I'm having problems with my congregation," he said. "Several of my parishioners have complained that I'm arrogant and over-critical. I don't see myself that way, but I'm beginning to wonder if they're right and I'm missing something."

"Why don't you take a temperament analysis test?" I suggested. "That might tell you something about the real you."

Grant agreed, so I gave him the Meyers-Briggs test. Upon tabulating the results, we found that he inwardly had a strong, compassionate concern for other people, but that he had real difficulty expressing this concern. He had simply never learned the skills to express caring for other people.

"Grant," I said, "I've grown to know you and love you as a friend and a brother. I've gotten the chance, on a number of occasions, to see the real love inside your heart. Now you've got to find some way to let your own parishioners see that love too. You've got to find some way to let them know you the way I know you."

Over the next few months, Grant and I met on a regular basis to talk about his life, and especially about his efforts to become more of an affirmer, less of an evaluator. He asked me to hold him accountable for his progress as, week by week, he took specific steps to show his genuine caring for different members of his congregation. He bought and read—no, devoured—books on leadership, encouragement, and pastoral caring. I watched him in group and individual situations as he worked to give more eye contact and other forms of nonverbal feedback to people when he talked to them.

Today, Grant is a transformed man. He still has streaks of the old evaluator in him, but if I were asked to label him as either an evaluator or an affirmer, I would unhesitatingly place him in the affirmer column.

No one is born an evaluator. No one is doomed to remain

critical for life. If you have a problem in this area, you can work on it. You can ask God to heal you of your critical tendencies and to replace your evaluating spirit with an affirming spirit. You can practice offering affirmation, acceptance, and encouragement to others instead of criticism. And you can ask your own mentor to hold you accountable, to check with you on your progress, to watch your behavior around others, and to bring it to your attention when you slip into a critical mode.

Does being an affirmer mean we never need to evaluate the behavior of others? Of course not. A mentoring relationship demands that the mentor be objective and honest with the learner. The mentor must be a mirror before the learner, reflecting the clear, cold light of truth. That means there will be hard times when tough things need to be said about specific areas of behavior in a learner. As mentors, we need the raw courage and honesty to be tough—yet we also need the sensitivity and commitment to be tender as well.

Tenderness *and* toughness? At the same time? Yes. At the same time.

Mentoring is not an "either/or" proposition—either tough or tender. Tenderness without toughness becomes a kind of sugary indulgence that smothers the learner's growth. Toughness without tenderness becomes harsh and cold, and leads to bitterness in the learner. Effective mentoring is "both/and"—*both* tender *and* tough.

"I WISH RON HAD CONFRONTED ME MORE"

Finding the right balance between tenderness and toughness has been a major struggle in my ministry and my mentoring relationships throughout my adult life. I have always found it much easier to be tender than tough. And when the people who know me best were interviewed for this book, they shared this perception of my personality: I need to add more toughness to my tenderness.

My friend Larry Olson, who learned youth ministry along-side me when I was an associate pastor in Minneapolis, re-flects, "Perhaps I could have learned more if Ron had been a little tougher on me, if he would have sat me down and evalu-ated my performance, if he had said, 'Here are your strengths, here are your weaknesses.' Ron wasn't strong on evaluating people. His strengths were motivating and encouraging peo-ple."

Today, some fifteen years after those Minneapolis days, Kemp Smeal, the music minister of the California church I cur-rently pastor, offers a nearly identical assessment. "Some of Ron's strengths," he says, "his grace and concern for people, can emerge as weaknesses in certain situations. One time, one of the church committees was proceeding in a certain direction on a certain issue. Ron felt the committee should move in a different direction, and he gently tried to communicate his feel-ings to the committee. Later, when the committee continued on its previously chosen course, he was frustrated and felt he hadn't been heard. As we talked about that situation not long ago, he said, 'I have to take a lot of the blame on that one. The poor communication was largely my fault. I should have stated my wishes more forcefully to the committee.'

"If Ron is disappointed in someone, he tends to repress it rather than address it. He's aware of that, and he's working on it. He's getting better about confronting when there's a need to confront."

What has surprised yet instructed me in the need for greater toughness in my mentoring relationships was hearing how much my friends *wanted* that toughness. Many times, people who were in mentoring relationships with me would say, "I'd like you to evaluate my performance in this area, Ron. I'd like you to honestly tell me how I'm doing." Yet, when a learner would disappoint me or make a mistake or fail in some area, I couldn't bring myself to point it out. I hated to make people feel bad, so I would just let the matter slide. I thought at the time I was being gracious, but now I think I was actually being cowardly.

Henry Chin recalls the years we served on the church board together in the early to mid-1980s: "At times, I wish Ron would have confronted me more, held me accountable more. Because he's so sensitive to others' feelings, he hates to challenge people. There were hard issues he and I should have faced together, but we didn't, primarily because it would have been awkward for me and Ron didn't want to place me in an awkward position. On the one hand, there is a gentleness to him that is very Christlike; yet on the other hand, it's often Christlike to confront."

Todd Treimer, who I've known since he was in junior high, observes, "Mercy is one of Ron's gifts. But a merciful person like Ron has trouble confronting people when there is sin in their life. So if I have one criticism of Ron, it is that he needs to be tougher in confronting people for their own good. As it says in Proverbs, 'more faithful are the wounds of a friend than the kisses of an enemy.' Oh, and one more criticism of Ron: he's a ball-hog on the basketball court. He needs to pass the ball around more."

(I accept the first criticism, but I *deny* hogging the ball!)

Mike Flavin relates the issue of tenderness and toughness to the opportunities I gave him to preach in my stead when we served on the same pastoral staff in the early 1980s: "Ron gave me opportunities to preach, sometimes to fill in when he was away or on vacation, but more often just to give me the practice and experience. He would often sit there on the platform, and I could feel him silently supporting me and praying for me while I preached. I was pretty green back then, and when I got through preaching, I knew it was lousy. But Ron could always pick out something positive in my sermon, and say, 'You really did this thing or that thing well.'

"Sure, there's a downside to a positive, encouraging nature like Ron's. There were a lot of times when he should have challenged me more, confronted me more. Ron majors so much on grace, that he has a tendency to cut a guy too much slack at times. But if a mentor has to err one way or the other, I think Ron errs in the right direction."

I hope Mike is right. I do believe that if a mentor must err one way or the other, it's better to err toward tenderness. Of course, it's always best not to err at all. As mentors, we should strive to find that Christlike, biblical balance between grace and accountability, between tenderness and toughness.

THE SEVEN CARDINAL RULES OF TENDER-TOUGH MENTORING

As we've seen, tenderness and toughness are complementary dimensions of effective mentoring. Without both dimensions, we cannot be complete as mentors. Let me suggest to you seven cardinal rules of tender-tough mentoring.

Rule #1: When You Confront, Be Honest and Direct.

Tenderness is not a matter of being diplomatic or tactful, of using euphemistic language, of "beating around the bush" and "softening the blow." Rather, we should say what needs to be said in clear and unmistakable terms. An effective mentor lays everything squarely on the line. As David Augsburger says, "If you love, you level."

A word of caution: I've seen people use words like "love" and "honesty" to disguise a multitude of sins. I've seen people screamed at, chewed up, and verbally abused in the name of "love." I've seen people ventilate their own anger at someone else in the name of "honesty."

Christopher was a young pastor, recently ordained to his first solo pastorate after having spent two years as an assistant pastor in another church. He entered his new job with exuberance, idealism, and a lot of fresh ideas.

Christopher's new ideas quickly brought him into conflict with Mr. and Mrs. Johnson. This couple had helped found the church thirty years earlier. Mr. Johnson had spent most of the last thirty years on the church board, and together with his wife, sat on the personnel committee which oversaw the four-member church staff.

According to the Johnsons, everything Christopher did was wrong. His preaching attracted too many new people to the small suburban church, and that, said the Johnsons, was "destroying the nice, intimate, homey atmosphere" they had always enjoyed. They objected to the contemporary music Christopher permitted in the worship service. They didn't like his use of humor in his preaching. They disagreed with minor theological points he raised. One week, they didn't think he did enough hospital visitation. Another week, they felt he spent too much time in visitation and not enough time in the church office.

The Johnsons criticized this young pastor at congregational meetings, confronted him at board meetings, shouted at him over the phone or in his office. In personnel meetings, they frequently threatened to fire him. Even though many people felt the Johnsons were wrong, few people had the courage to stand up to them in support of their new pastor.

During one meeting of the personnel committee, the Johnsons, as usual, pressed the attack against their harried young pastor. Mr. Johnson opened his briefcase and pulled out a document, ten pages long, neatly typed, single spaced. He had made photocopies for the entire committee, including Christopher himself. "This," said Mr. Johnson, "is a list I have compiled of all our pastor's shortcomings. I would like him to answer each of these charges. And if he does not answer to our satisfaction, I will expect this committee to call for his resignation."

Just then, Mr. Clark, one of the other committee members, stood, took his copy of Mr. Johnson's list, and tore it down the middle. "Brother Johnson," said Mr. Clark, "the whole church knows how you feel about our pastor. Unfortunately, the whole church—myself included—has been too spineless to tell you what we think about the way you have treated him. I'm ashamed of the fact that I have just sat by, month after month, while you and your wife have made life miserable for this godly young man."

"Brother Clark," said Mr. Johnson, a look of surprise and hurt on his face, "all we have tried to do is to be honest with our pastor. We love him enough to tell him the truth about what he's doing wrong, so he can change. The problem is that we have loved him and loved him and loved him, and he *still* refuses to change!"

Mr. Johnson was not being dishonest with Mr. Clark. But he was being dishonest with himself. He had convinced himself that this constant barrage of criticism and opposition he and his wife had leveled at their pastor was an act of "honesty" and "love." The truth was that they had become bitterly, unalterably opposed to their pastor, and they sought to rationalize and sanctify their hostility by labeling it "love."

None of us is qualified to confront until we have carefully, honestly searched our own motivations for doing so—including, as much as humanly possible, those motivations that evade our conscious minds. As mentors, we should always confront with reluctance, never with eagerness. We should confront honestly, directly, yet gently, and always with a genuine desire to bring about God's best in the other person's life. It is far more Christlike to confront another person through tears of sorrow than with a voice raised in anger.

Rule #2: When You Confront, Demonstrate Unconditional Love and Acceptance.

Our tough honesty should be covered with tender caring, affirmation, and an unconditional commitment both to the learner and to the mentoring relationship. Let's say you are a mentor to a young woman named Janice who works alongside you in the business you own. You notice she has a problem dealing with your customers. She doesn't mean to offend people, and she isn't even aware that she does so; yet there is an abruptness in her manner that puts people off. What would be the tender-tough approach to making Janice aware of this problem?

A lot of people might take Janice aside and immediately start trying to smooth things over. "Janice, there's something I need to talk to you about. But first, I want you to know that I think you're really doing a great job. You're so organized and efficient. I don't know when the files have been in better shape. Oh, and you sure did a bang-up job on the advertising flyer last week. Even the typing was first-rate." And on and on, a long list of compliments.

The problem with this scenario is that Janice knows you didn't take her aside just to heap a lot of praise on her. She knows that, in a few moments, you're going to make a transition with the word *but* or *however* and then the other shoe will drop. All the while you are reciting the litany of her accomplishments, Janice is growing more wary, more defensive, more impatient, knowing that some unpleasantness is about to hit her right between the eyes. Instead of softening the blow, you are keeping her in suspense, increasing her inner tension.

That's not the "tender toughness" of authentic biblical mentoring. That's just a timid reluctance to get to the point.

So where does the tenderness come in? Just listen to this approach: "Janice, I've got something to tell you. I know this won't be easy for either of us, but I respect you enough to give it to you straight. I care about you, I'm committed to our relationship, and I want you to be the best you can be for Jesus Christ. Janice, the problem is there's something in your manner that sometimes puts people off. You tend to be a bit abrupt at times, and some folks interpret that as unfriendliness. I know you don't mean it that way, and that you're probably not even aware of it. That's why I felt I needed to bring it to your attention."

Do you see the tenderness there? There's no sugar coating on these words. On the contrary, these words are clear and unambiguous. Janice is not left feeling she's been "set up" with a lot of compliments, only to be "shot down" later with criticism. Instead, she feels respected and cared for. She knows it wasn't easy for you to confront her, but that you performed this act of loving toughness because you are committed to the relationship and to her growth. Most importantly, she knows she is accepted and loved, regardless of her faults and failings.

Paul Tournier, the Swiss Christian psychologist who has been a tender-tough mentor to hundreds of people around the world, was interviewed a few years ago. When the interviewer asked him to explain his counseling techniques, Tournier replied, "It's a little embarrassing for me, having all these students coming from all over the world to study my 'techniques,' for they always go away disappointed. All I have learned to do is simply accept people right in the midst of their struggles." That's the minimum guarantee we as mentors should make to those who are learning from us: No matter what they do or how grievously they fail, we will unconditionally accept and love them.

Rule #3: When You Confront, Be Specific. Never Generalize.

In your confrontation of Janice it would be important to specify times when you noticed her abruptness. You wouldn't simply say, "You're always abrupt and unfriendly." Rather, you would say, "You were abrupt with Mrs. Jones yesterday. She came up to me later and asked, 'Whatever did I say to offend Janice?' I had to tell her not to take it personally, that you are really a warm and friendly person, but that it doesn't always show."

When you generalize about a person's character, faults, or habits, they usually become defensive. And understandably so. Such generalizations sound and feel like an attack on *who a person is* instead of a constructive reproof on *what a person does*. Moreover, the vagueness of such generalizations doesn't give the learner a clue what he or she should do to grow and change. But if you refer to specific behaviors and events, the learner has something tangible to react to and work on.

Rule #4: When You Confront, Demonstrate Empathy.

Put yourself in the learner's place. Remember what you went through when you were at the learner's level of skill and maturity. Remember the ways people confronted you when you failed—particularly those who were in authority over you or who were your mentors. Then, think about how you *wish* they had confronted you.

One of the most important characteristics of an effective mentor is the ability to put ourselves in the learner's place. As novelist John Erskine once observed, "We have not really budged a step until we've taken up residence in someone else's point of view."

Some time ago, I was called upon to confront a staff member about his work. So I went to his office—not merely as the senior pastor but as a mentor and friend—and I laid out the areas where he was failing to perform as he should. It was very hard for both of us, and we both became teary-eyed as we talked.

"I want you to know that I'm your advocate, not your adversary," I told him. "I just wish you knew how much I want you to become a success in this job."

"I know that," he said. "I really do. I just have a hard time processing criticism. I get caught up in a shame spiral, going back all the way to when I was a kid. I never felt valued in my family. I was always being criticized and told how useless and stupid I was. I guess I just give too much power to criticism."

Remembering that my family was away from home that evening, I invited this young man to dinner. We spent a lot of time talking; then we went to a movie. That night, I learned a lot about this young man's family background, his areas of brokenness, his needs, his hurts.

It's easy for a mentor to fall into a "checklist relationship" with the learner—to run through the list and say, "Please do better in this and this and this." What is harder—and infinitely more effective—is to demonstrate empathy, to really get involved in the learner's life, to understand his or her inner spiritual and emotional reality. Our primary concern in a mentoring relationship should not be, "Did you get the job done?" but, "Are you becoming a whole person in Christ?"

Rule #5: Build on the Learner's Strengths, Gifts, and Character Through Positive Encouragement.

Earn the right to confront. Make sure that you affirm the learner 97 percent of the time, so that when it's time to be tough in the remaining three percent, your tender caring and affirmation will be credible. How will the learner know you're on his or her side if the only evaluation you ever pass on is a negative one?

Kemp Smeal, the music minister of our church, offers this reflection on our mentoring relationship: "Ron is a 'wind beneath my wings' mentor—the kind of friend and encourager who lifts you up and teaches you to fly solo. He builds you up publicly. He spends time with you privately, cementing the friendship, making you feel valued. Then, in those times when he has to objectively evaluate or criticize your performance, he does so with grace, with a genuine concern for the individual."

Rule #6: Affirm in Public, Correct in Private.

The goal of mentoring is to build up, not to tear down. If you rebuke a person in public, you bring humiliation, embarrassment, and shame on him or her. You destroy self-esteem. You set the mentoring process back.

But when you affirm in public, you build self-esteem, confidence, and incentive. Of course, that affirmation should be realistic and honest, not just empty words of praise. By affirming sincerely and publicly, you plant the seeds of greatness in the learner.

"Ron confronts me when I need it," says my associate, Peter Hiett, "but he always does so graciously and in private. Publicly, he always builds me up. As important as skills are, Ron emphasizes building character and emotional wholeness more than building skills. I try to emulate that emphasis in my own mentoring relationships with others."

Rule #7: Build an Allegiance to Relationships, Not to Issues.

I've found that people generally tend to build an allegiance to relationships or to issues. That is, people tend to become primarily concerned about other people and their feelings and quality of the relationship, or they become focused on rules, agendas, quotas, tasks, and results. The effective mentor always puts relationships ahead of issues.

My father was that kind of mentor, both in his own family and in the church he pastored for twenty-five years. Many times I heard him say, "The individual is always more important than the issue." He lived this principle daily, and he built it into my life. Today, I try to pass on this principle to others.

You can differ with other people, and sometimes you must even confront other people, but no matter how intense the conflict between yourself and another, that person should never leave your presence feeling devalued or unloved. One comment I hear over and over from people who knew my dad: "He always made me feel valued and special."

Dad made me feel valued and special as his son too. Once, when I was about thirteen years old, my brother Paul and I did something that made my dad very angry. He shouted at us both, then stormed out of the house and slammed the door. This was entirely out of character for this very even-tempered man. In fact, I never saw my dad so angry before that time or since.

Our house was right across from the church my dad pastored. I remember looking out our front window after he left the house and seeing him open the door of the church and go inside. It was two hours or more before he emerged from that darkened, empty sanctuary. I don't know what he did in there all that time, but I suspect he spent those hours in prayer.

I was in bed before my dad came home, but I couldn't sleep. I was miserable because I had caused this gentle man to lose his temper in a way I had never before witnessed. As I lay there feeling utterly wretched, my bedroom door swung slowly open. There was my dad. He hesitated a moment, then came in and knelt at my bedside. "Ron," he whispered, "are you awake?"

"I'm awake," I said. "Dad, I'm awful sorry—"

"I know you are, son," he said. "But I wanted to tell you I'm sorry too. I was wrong to yell at you like that. Please forgive me."

He was asking *me* to forgive *him!* This act of love and reconciliation is as alive today as it was then, for it's alive in my memory and in my heart. It's one of many memories of my dad that continues to guide me in my own family and mentoring relationships.

Picture this scenario: You are in a mentoring relationship with Tom, an employee of your company. You are seeking to pass on to him not only your business acumen, but your Christian character and ethical principles. He is learning by shared experience how a Christian businessman treats customers, suppliers, and employees. One day, Tom makes a mistake which costs the company several thousand dollars. How do you respond? Do you lash out at Tom? Fire him? Make an example of him? Is your allegiance to the issue of a major dollar loss, or is your allegiance to Tom, to his maturity, to helping him learn and grow from his mistake without being broken by it?

Obviously, I'm not suggesting that a person who habitually makes careless and costly mistakes should be allowed to run a business into the ground. There must be accountability in every enterprise, be it in a company, a ministry, a church, or a family. But within that overall framework of accountability, there must be some freedom to fail and to make mistakes. And the mentoring relationship must always come before any issue.

Or picture this: You are in a mentoring relationship with Laura, an intern on your church staff. The more you get to know Laura, the more you realize she holds a lot of ideas with which you disagree. Her political views are 180 degrees out of phase with yours. She opposes the spending of all that money on a new Christian Education wing, even though you're the chairman of the building program. Are you going to get along with Laura, be a mentor to her, pray for her, and encourage her in her work in the church? Or will your differences break the relationship? Is your allegiance to the issues that separate you or to the mentoring relationship that binds you together as mentor and learner?

AFFECTION: THE CORNERSTONE OF
TENDER-TOUGH MENTORING

The concept of building an allegiance to relationships can be summed up under one word: *affection*. Open the New Testament and the intense affection of Jesus shines from the pages. He didn't just preach to people; he was with them and among them. They touched him, and he touched them. He wept over them and hurt with them. His heart was broken over those who were sick or in pain or in poverty.

You see this same affection for people in the apostle Paul. He expressed it clearly and eloquently in all his letters. When he reminded the Thessalonian Christians that he was gentle among them, "just as a nursing mother cherishes her own children,"[1] I'm reminded of the gentle care my wife, Shirley, has lavished on our children—how she hurt for them when they were sick, or how her face beamed when they performed in the school program.

You can hear the deep affection of Paul as he reminded the Corinthians how he had written to them "with many tears . . . that you might know the love which I have so abundantly for you."[2] To Timothy, to whom he was such an important mentor and guide, Paul wrote, "I remember you . . . greatly desiring to see you, . . . that I may be filled with joy. . . . Be diligent to come to me quickly."[3] Genuine affection for people was at the heart of the mentoring process of the apostle Paul.

Over the years, one of the most rewarding and mutual mentoring relationships in my life has been with a man named Bob Osborne. Bob is co-manager of the First Presbyterian Thrift Shop in Fresno, California, and a man with a tender heart for people. He has traveled to Africa and India to see human need firsthand and to do whatever he can to meet those needs. Bob doesn't think of himself as a missionary, but, instead, as an ordinary Christian in an ordinary American church, who happens to care about suffering people. I have stood with Bob in the dusty street of an African village and seen tears roll down his face because his heart was broken over the misery of men, women, and little children devastated by ground-cracking famine.

On one trip to India, Bob stuffed into his suitcase as many shoes as would fit. Why? Because shoes are a rare commodity in India, and he planned to leave as many pairs as possible with his poor Indian brothers and sisters. On the return flight, Bob was barefooted. He had taken the shoes off his own feet to give to an Indian farmer.

When my co-author, Jim Denney, talked to Bob about our mentoring relationship, Bob gave his perspective on the tender-tough relationship he and I had shared together. "A lot of the things I've learned from Ron are hard to put into words," he said. "They're not so much lessons as they are *experiences*. One of those experiences was in a hospital room, shortly before the death of one of our pastors, Ted Lyons. One moment we were joking and reminiscing with Ted, the next moment we were praying together. Sometimes, Ron just cried with Ted, hugged him, and told him how much he loved him.

"I'll always admire and remember Ron's love, and his consistency in maintaining close relationships with people, his demonstrations of affection. I'm trying to build those qualities into my own relationships.

"Right now, I'm working with Asian high school students, children of Southeast Asian refugees. These young people have a lot of questions about our culture and our way of life. From Ron, I learned a lot about the empathy you need to help people from another culture find a new life. I try to put myself in their place."

Unconditional love, positive encouragement, empathy, affirmation, and a willingness to face specific areas head on—these are indispensable ingredients for an effective, tender-tough mentoring relationship. But the cornerstone of effective mentoring—the ingredient which is so often overlooked—is the ingredient of *affection*.

STEEL AND VELVET

Carl Sandburg had an expression that poetically captures the meaning of tender toughness: "steel and velvet." On the 150th anniversary of the birthday of Abraham Lincoln, Sandburg stood before a joint assembly of Congress and gave an address entitled, "Lincoln: Man of Steel and Velvet." Here is an excerpt of Sandberg's description of Lincoln, delivered February 12, 1959:

> Not often in the story of mankind does one arrive on the earth who is both steel and velvet, who is as hard as rock and soft as the drifting fog, who holds in his heart and mind the paradox of terrible storm and peace unspeakable.
>
> While the war winds howled, he insisted that the Mississippi was one river meant to belong to one country; that railroad connections from coast to coast must be pushed through while war wavered and broke and came again; as generals failed and campaigns were lost, he held enough forces of the North together to raise new armies and supply them until new generals could be found. In the mixed shame and blame of the immense wrongs of two clashing civilizations, often with nothing to say, he said nothing.
>
> During those days he would sleep not at all and, on occasion, he was seen to weep in a way that made weeping appropriate, decent, majestic.

Lincoln, a man of steel and velvet. Yet, as great a man as Lincoln was, there was another man who even more perfectly exemplified what it means to be both tender and tough. The quintessential Man of Steel and Velvet was also the quintessential mentor, Jesus Christ.

THE QUINTESSENTIAL MAN OF STEEL
AND VELVET

A man of steel, Jesus confronted the religious evil of his day. He called the corrupt religious leaders vipers, hypocrites, white-washed tombs full of dead bones. Like steel, he cleared the moneychangers out of the Temple. Like steel, he confronted Peter, told him he could be a rock, that he should be consistent, that he should stop wavering.

Yet it was a man of velvet who wept over the death of his friend Lazarus. It was the velvet in the man that gave him compassion for a woman caught in adultery. It was the velvet in him that led him to reach out to the little children who crowded around him. It was the velvet in him that compelled him, just hours before the Cross, to kneel before his disciples and wash their feet.

Our task as mentors is to imitate the Master Mentor, Jesus himself. Our lives must be marked both with Christ's toughness and his tenderness, both his steel and his velvet. This means that those of us who are tender Christians will have to become a bit more tough, and those of us who are tough will have to learn a little more tenderness.

The tender Christian who avoids building toughness into his or her life soon becomes little more than a weak sentimentalist. The tough Christian who has no use for tenderness inevitably hardens into a harshly critical Pharisee. To be Christlike mentors, we must have these complementary qualities in dynamic balance in our lives.

If we are to be conformed into the image of Christ, we must allow Christ to mold and reshape our character. We must invite him to put a reinforcing rod of steel into our backbone so that we can live out his strength. We must allow him to reupholster our hard surfaces and rough edges with velvet so that we can live out his love and compassion.

Even as we seek to mentor others, we must never cease to be learners at the feet of the Master Mentor himself.

Chapter 5

THE MENTOR AND FAILURE

Failure is as important as success

FAILURE HAS VALUE

In the spring of 1979, the nation's worst nuclear accident took place at Three Mile Island, near Harrisburg, Pennsylvania. One of the top managers of the power plant at the time of the accident was later reprimanded for failing to provide an adequate response to the crisis. Then he was demoted and reassigned to the power company's fossil fuels division.

Question: Is this the best way to deal with failure? When someone makes a serious mistake, should we punish that person and exile that person to a place where he or she can never make the same mistake again?

The response to this incident typifies the corporate attitude toward failure in the 1960s, 1970s, and most of the 1980s: "One mistake, and you're out." This resulted in an increasingly staid and stagnant managerial outlook during those decades. Executives and employees took the attitude that risk should be avoided at all costs, while mistakes should be covered up or blamed on subordinates. No one was ever allowed to learn and grow from his or her mistakes. America's reputation as a bold, daring, innovative society began to decline.

Sometime during the 1980s, a change gradually took place as the American business community awakened to the fact that *failure has value*. Employees who would have been sacked for a big blunder in bygone days now found they were given the chance to stick with the job, learn from their mistakes, and fix them.

If America were to experience another similar nuclear accident, perhaps the discipline for the employee responsible would be handled differently. Perhaps the person in charge of the nuclear facility would be given the opportunity to correct his error and to become an *expert* on how to manage such crises. Perhaps this person would even be given the opportunity to train others in how to avoid the mistakes he or she made. When people are given the opportunity to learn and grow from their mistakes, their failures can become as valuable to them as their successes.

During the early 1980s, when Steven Jobs was running Apple Computers and the company was reaping three-quarters of a billion dollars a year in sales, a reporter asked Jobs, "How does Apple do it?" Jobs's reply: "We hire really great people and we create an environment where people can make mistakes and grow."

In their classic study of America's best-managed corporations, *In Search of Excellence,* Thomas J. Peters and Robert H. Waterman wrote about the positive role failure often plays in achieving ultimate success.

A special attribute of the success-oriented, positive, and innovating environment is a substantial tolerance for failure. James Burke [chief executive officer of Johnson & Johnson] says one of J&J's tenets is that "you've got to be willing to fail." He adds that General Johnson, J&J's founder, said to him, "If I wasn't making mistakes, I wasn't making decisions." Emerson's Charles Knight argues: "You need the ability to fail. You cannot innovate unless you are willing to accept mistakes." Tolerance for failure is a very specific part of the excellent company culture—and that lesson comes directly from the top. Champions have to make lots of tries and consequently suffer some failures or the organization won't learn.[1]

No one wants to fail. You don't admire failure, and neither do I. I'm sure you and I both believe we should never offer God anything less than our best. When interviewed by Jim Denney, Kemp Smeal said, "One dimension of Ron's character that especially appeals to me as a musician is his commitment to excellence. Yet, as important as excellence and competence are to him, he never puts stellar performance ahead of people's needs or feelings."

Excellence is important, but our need to risk, to learn from our mistakes, and to grow spiritually and emotionally is even more important. So while I would never recommend failure as a way of life, I have to confess that failure has value. It's a fact: Most of us learn more from our failures than from our successes.

THE FAILURE OF THE TWELVE

Failure has a special place of importance in the mentoring process. We see it clearly displayed in the mentoring relationship between Jesus and the Twelve. On the night Jesus was betrayed, just before the crucifixion, he was with the Twelve in the Upper Room. And when you read the account of that night in all four gospels, you readily find that what was going on in that Upper Room didn't bear much resemblance to the haloed, idealized images of the Last Supper we find in paintings by da Vinci and Tintoretto.

These twelve men were bickering, arguing, insulting each other, each claiming to be the greatest in the kingdom, the greatest of Jesus' disciples. While they were arguing, they heard something in the background: the sound of water being poured into a basin. The clash of voices died as Jesus knelt before his friends and quietly began washing their feet. But when Jesus got to Peter with his basin and towel, Peter remonstrated, "You shall never wash my feet!"

At first glance, you might think Peter was demonstrating great humility, as if he were saying, "Jesus, I'm not worthy to have you wash my feet." But that's not what was on Peter's mind at all. As Charles Swindoll reflected in his book *Improving Your Serve,* "Peter wasn't about to be that vulnerable. After all, Jesus was the Master. No way was he going to wash the dirt off Peter's feet! I ask you, is that humility? You know it's not."[2] Peter was saying, in effect, "Jesus, I don't need your help. My feet aren't dirty. Go ahead and wash these other guys' feet, but I'm doing just fine."

Perhaps you can identify with Peter. I can. It's hard to admit that we have dirty feet. It's hard to admit we have need, sin, and failure in our lives.

After Jesus washed the feet of the Twelve and celebrated the Passover with them, Jesus led his friends out to the Mount of Olives to pray. There he predicted his own arrest and the failure and defection of the Twelve. Again, Peter proudly spoke up: "If I have to die with you, I will not deny you." And, of course, we know the result of Peter's declaration. He defected, he denied his Lord, he failed his friend and mentor, Jesus.

But failure wasn't the end of Peter's story. Following the Resurrection, Jesus was reunited with his friend Peter by the Sea of Galilee. All of Peter's former pride was erased, replaced by a contrite and shame-filled humility. But Jesus, the Master Mentor, did not leave his friend Peter in his shame. Knowing that failure has value, Jesus forgave and restored Peter, charging him with a massive responsibility: "Feed my sheep." Despite his failure, Peter was given the awesome job of shepherding the new community called the church. As writer Stephen Shores observed,

> Could God forgive such a colossal failure? Was Peter even worth the try? Are we? Yes! . . . Peter found himself not only forgiven but trusted. He learned that failure is not the ultimate.
>
> Failure is the unforgivable sin in American culture—so much so that it often paralyzes the individual in a deep-freeze of depression, self-condemnation, and resignation. The Bible, though, is full of the idea that our failures are not irreversible in their effects. Peter failed utterly but not ultimately, for God used him as an awesome force in the early Church. Our Father's ability to forgive and restore far outweighs our capacity for failure.[3]

Failure was not the end of Peter's career. It was the beginning. Jesus knew that Peter had earned a doctorate in Christian humility—the hard way. This made Peter vastly more valuable to the kingdom than if he had never experienced the shame of his failure.

As mentors, we must believe in the learner. That means that when the learner fails and falls, we don't turn our backs on him. Instead, we are there to lift him, dust him off, and reinstate him, just as Jesus reinstated Peter. Failure does not destroy the worth of the human being; usually, it enhances it.

THE QUINTESSENTIAL MAN OF FAILURE

The most compelling portrait of failure is found in Isaiah 53:2–3. It is a portrait of Jesus Christ. This messianic passage from the Old Testament describes Jesus in this way:

> *He has no form or comeliness;*
> *And when we see Him,*

> *There is no beauty*
> *   that we should desire Him.*
> *He is despised and rejected by men,*
> *A Man of sorrows*
> *   and acquainted with grief.*
> *And we hid, as it were,*
> *   our faces from Him;*
> *He was despised,*
> *   and we did not esteem Him.*

Jesus was, in short, a failure. He had no achievements. He had no honors. He had no titles or degrees.

What did Jesus ever accomplish in his lifetime? He was born in the middle of nowhere, the son of an unwed teenage girl. He gathered around him a group of illiterate rabble-rousers who followed him as he wandered the countryside for three years. At the end of that time, one of his followers turned him in to the authorities and he was hauled off and executed like a thief. As he was being dragged off to face the Cross, his so-called friends deserted him and left him to die. His cause was ended. As he hung from that cross of shame, bleeding and broken, people laughed derisively and said to each other, "How could this *failure* save anybody?"

Yet, as Jesus hung upon the cross, a failure for all the world to see and scorn, he did nothing less than *conquer* sin and *disarm* death. He exploded from the tomb and ascended in resurrection power. He transformed failure into victory.

As Peter Marshall once wrote, "It is better to fail in a cause that will ultimately succeed than to succeed in a cause that will ultimately fail." Our resurrected Lord is proof of that statement. As we look ahead to the ultimate victory of Jesus Christ over the fallen systems of this world, we draw strength and encouragement from the fact that this same Jesus has already led the way through failure and despair.

In his mentoring relationship with his friend Peter—a bumbling, sinful, failure-prone human being so much like you and me—we see that Jesus stands ready to use failure to change us and make us all we were meant to be in him.

FAILURE IS AN EDUCATION

Whether you and I are in the role of learner or mentor, this is one lesson we need to learn: Failure is not the end. Failure is an education.

Glen Early was young but highly ambitious when he founded his construction company in Harrisonburg, Virginia. Within two years, the company was broke and Early, only twenty-five years old, was thousands of dollars in debt. That was in 1975. Unwilling to declare bankruptcy, he mortgaged his home to pay off his creditors. Then he apprenticed himself to the owner of a thriving construction firm in the area.

Working alongside this very successful businessman, Early saw how such procedures as contracting, estimating, and bidding *should* be carried out, versus how he *had* carried them out. During this time he also took college courses in business administration.

Armed with a fresh store of maturity, knowledge, and experience, Early founded a new construction company in 1982. Six years later, Early's firm was listed in *Inc.* magazine as one of the country's fastest-growing entrepreneurial enterprises. Had he not failed in his first business attempt, however, he never would have gone back to do the "homework"—both in school and on the job—which made success possible. Glen Early understands the value of failure. He has wisely learned to view failure not as a dead end but as a beginning.

The Chinese ideogram for *crisis* consists of two characters, one which means "danger" and another which means "opportunity." The wise mentor learns to find the opportunity embedded in every crisis of failure, and he helps others learn to do the same.

I would encourage you, as a mentor, to be open about your own failures with the person who is learning from you, especially at those times when he or she needs to hear that failure is not the end. If, for example, that learner has just lost his or her job, share about a time you got fired from a job. Think back to those feelings of failure and battered self-confidence. Empathize and encourage that person that you've been there too and that you've rebounded and overcome your setbacks.

A biblical mentor seeks to live a life-style of complete transparency before the learner, never hesitating to share past mistakes or bad decisions within an atmosphere of confidence and trust. To admit we were wrong yesterday is just another way of saying we are wiser today.

When he was hired as our youth pastor, the transparency of our church staff was a great encouragement to Peter Hiett: "I had just graduated from Fuller Seminary, and I was anxious and a little insecure. I wondered, *Can I match up to the other people on this staff?* I was introduced to the staff and we met together for a time of prayer and getting acquainted.

"Ron began by saying, 'We're all broken people here. We all have needs and hurts. But God is able to use us in our weakness. So I'd like to open our time together by going around the room and each of us sharing just one area of hurt or weakness in his or her life.'

"Ron led in a very vulnerable way by expressing some of his own feelings of insecurity. Then, one by one, everyone else in the room confessed an area of weakness. I was thunderstruck to see how open and humble the staff of this church was. I no longer had to worry about measuring up. In that room, with those people, I had the freedom to be myself. We're all broken people, and I've learned from Ron that the way of healing begins with the honest confession of our brokenness."

That's the liberating power of honesty and vulnerability in mentoring relationships. False facades of self-sufficiency and easy success are not only dishonest but destructive to the mentoring process. What is there to be learned from a mentor who seems to breeze effortlessly through life?

The value of the mentoring process lies in watching a person of genuine wisdom and character surmount obstacles, solve problems, and overcome mistakes. The secret to profoundly influencing others as a mentor lies in honestly, transparently opening our lives for inspection, warts and all.

One way to do this is to open your home to others. Beginning shortly after our marriage and continuing to the present day, Shirley and I have made a point of opening our home, particularly to people in their late teens or twenties. An unwed expectant mother. Church staff members. High school and college students. Interns. Friends seeking to establish themselves in a new job or new community.

For a period of a week to a number of months, that person lives in our home, sharing meals and family times with us, watching how Shirley and I deal with our children, watching us handle stress, conflict, and emergencies, observing how we try and fail and then try again—in short, discovering how we live out our faith in the trenches of everyday life.

When someone is living within those same four walls with you, it's pretty hard to keep up a false front. The reality of who you are—the good, the bad, and the ugly—is bound to emerge.

And that's what mentoring is all about: not teaching idealized theories, but living out reality on a daily basis. Even the reality of failure.

Chapter 6

INTEGRITY
You've got to walk your talk

REMINISCING ON THE RUN

The sunlight slanted over the Rockies, painting the trees, the ground, and the houses with a warm golden glow. My brother Paul and I were jogging on the running trails that wound among the hills west of Denver, near the Red Rocks Amphitheatre. It was 1984, and I remember the scene clearly: the dirt paths beaten down by the shoes of many other runners, the hilly and wooded countryside, the stands of brush where the deer would pause and stare in amazement as these strange human creatures loped by.

Paul and I ran this ten-mile course every evening during our stay with his family. It was a good time to be alone with my brother. We took the course at an easy pace, and we talked as we ran. We talked about a lot of things, but mostly reminisced. About the days when we were growing up together in Iowa. About the good times we had. About our dad. About our faith in Christ.

"Ron," Paul said as we pounded down a gently sloping grade, "you and I are both following Christ. There are so many

wrong turns we could have taken in our lives. A lot of choices,
a lot of temptations. But we're still following Jesus—just like
Mom and Dad used to pray we would when we were kids. Why
do you think that is?"

I thought about it for a few strides. "Aside from the influence of the Holy Spirit," I said at last, "and just from a human
perspective, I'd have to say it's the way Mom and Dad lived."

"What way is that?"

"They lived what they said they believed," I replied. "The
things Dad preached in the pulpit, the things they both taught
us at home, the times they disciplined us—it all matched up
with the way they lived."

"Right," said Paul, huffing slightly as we started up a hill.
"I thought that's what you'd say. Integrity. Walking your talk.
When kids see that in their parents, they want to live that way
too. Dad was the finest man I ever knew. He always lived what
he believed. I want to be that kind of dad to my boys."

And Paul was that kind of dad.

I try to be that kind of dad to my own children too.

CONGRUENCE: YOUR WALK = YOUR TALK

Integrity may be defined as the congruence—that is, consistency, harmony, agreement—between one's walk and one's
talk. In my father's life, in my mother's life, there was
integrity—a total congruence between what they said and how
they lived. I have grown up admiring that in my parents. I want
to be like that.

Shirley and I keep the goal of personal integrity before us as
we raise and mentor our own children. Sure, we're human,
we're flawed, we fail—but the goal of a fully integrated inner
and outer life is there. I often ask myself, "Will my daughter
and son see the kind of consistency and integrity in my life that
will cause them to want my values and my faith? Will the people who work alongside me see that consistency in me? Will
my friends, my neighbors, and my community see that in me?"

Some years ago, a father received a letter from his college-aged son which read in part, "Hey, Pop! This letter is free. They didn't cancel the stamp on your last letter to me, so I used it again."

A few days later, the son received a letter from his father. When he unfolded the letter, he found a stamp pasted at the top with a big, bold X drawn through it. Beneath the stamp, the father had written, "Dear Son, your debt to the United States Government has been paid."

Here was a father mentoring his son in the meaning of integrity.

Integrity is an essential ingredient of every mentor's life. As a mentor, you are being watched, weighed, tested, and imitated. If there is hypocrisy in your life, if there is any disparity between what you say and how you live, those who are watching your life will either be disillusioned or led into the same error you are living.

THE FOOLISH WISE MAN

King Solomon was a wise man, a mentor not only to his sons and to those who served under him, but to the whole nation of Israel. His thoughts, his values, his achievements were reflected in the spirit and accomplishments of the nation. The splendor of King Solomon became the splendor of Israel. The reputation of King Solomon became the reputation of Israel. And the folly of King Solomon became Israel's downfall.

Solomon constructed an immense temple to the Lord, made of stone and cedar overlaid with gold, at a cost that would probably exceed 5 billion dollars in 1990s dollars. He built a massive navy and ruled during the most peaceful and affluent period of Israel's history. He composed 3,000 proverbs and 1,005 songs, which comprise three books of the Old Testament.

After Solomon had built the Temple, God appeared to him and promised him,

Now if you walk before Me . . . in integrity *of heart and in*
uprightness, to do according to all that I have commanded
you, and if you keep My statutes and My judgments, then I
will establish the throne of your kingdom over Israel for-
ever. . . . But if you or your sons at all turn from following Me,
and do not keep My commandments and My statutes which I
have set before you, but go and serve other gods and worship
them, then I will cut off Israel from the land which I have
given them (emphasis added).[1]

But Solomon didn't walk with integrity of heart and in uprightness.

Despite all his wisdom and achievements for God, he began
to compromise and flirt with the evil of the world. His magnifi-
cent reign came under a cloud. Seduced by his own baser instincts and the attentions of foreign women who worshiped
other gods, Solomon wandered in his heart from the decrees
and laws of God. The wise man who had built the Temple of
God now became a fool, building altars to false gods. Tragically, King Solomon reinstated the idolatry his father David
had driven out of Israel.

Solomon's lack of integrity contaminated his son Rehoboam, whom Solomon was mentoring and training to succeed
him as king. Although Solomon had spent many hours with
Rehoboam, teaching him wisdom, faith, obedience to God, the
duties of leadership, when Rehoboam took up the crown of
Israel following Solomon's apostasy and death, he proceeded
to take Israel even deeper into error and idolatry. The promis-
ing young prince became a cruel and hated despot. The once-
prosperous nation of Israel fell into poverty, turmoil, and war.
Only five years into Rehoboam's reign, the once-glorious Temple built by his father Solomon was plundered and desecrated.

That is a lesson that all of us—not only as parents, but as
mentors and leaders—should take to heart: When we fail to

walk with integrity, we contaminate the generations that follow us. I've seen the devastating effect of this solemn principle in the lives of contemporary Christians. I've seen it in the headlines and in the lives of people very close to me.

HEADING FOR A CRASH

Some years ago, there was a story on the news about a bizarre tragedy involving a private jet. Aboard the jet were the pilot and one passenger. During its flight, air traffic controllers noticed that the plane was off its flight plan, and the pilot was not responding to radio calls. The plane followed a straight, high-altitude path across several states and finally out over the ocean. It was tracked by radar until it spent its fuel and fell into the sea.

Though the exact cause of the crash remains a mystery to this day, air safety investigators concluded that the plane must have lost cabin pressure during the flight. Deprived of oxygen, both pilot and passenger either died or fell unconscious. Meanwhile, the plane's autopilot kept the plane on a straight-line course, kept the wings trimmed, just as if it were being consciously piloted, until the fuel ran out and the inevitable crash occurred. Anyone happening to look up and see that jet passing high overhead would have noticed nothing out of the ordinary.

But even though everything about the plane seemed normal on the outside, something was seriously wrong on the inside.

You and I are just like that plane if there is an area in our lives where we lack integrity. We can cruise on autopilot, glide smoothly along, seemingly on a straight course, our wings trimmed and level. But if God is not in total control of our inner being, then we are headed for a crash.

So many people are depending on us, watching us, drawing strength and encouragement from our example. If we lack integrity, it is not just ourselves, but all these other people who will get hurt. When a mentor crashes, he takes a lot of people with him.

Those of us who are in business need to consider how we are modeling Christian integrity before our employees and associates. What do the bookkeeper, the accountant, and the junior executives learn from the way we deal with the company ledger, the tax forms, the accounts payable and receivable? Do they see someone who demonstrates integrity in every matter, whether it involves a dollar or a million dollars? Whether it involves an employee, a client, or the IRS? Do they see someone who operates with complete integrity regarding the use of office supplies, a company car, the copier, or the fax machine?

Not long ago, I learned to my dismay that a Christian businessman whom I have respected and admired was caught misusing his expense account. He took his wife out to dinner, then charged it off as a business entertainment expense. He and his wife took vacation trips, then charged them off as business trips.

I submit that if you, as a business person, are operating on the basis of complete integrity, then when you leave the office at the end of the day, you should be able to empty your pockets and not find so much as a paper clip belonging to the company. If you have integrity in the smallest details, you will never fall to a major temptation.

INTEGRITY OFTEN PAYS

Robert George is a businessman who understands the meaning of integrity. His story appeared in the August 1987 issue of *Nation's Business*. The CEO of Medallion Construction Company in Merrimack, New Hampshire, George is often invited to bid on multi-million dollar projects for the federal government. On one such occasion, as he was assembling a bid for a $2.5 million housing project, he received an estimate from a subcontractor that was $30,000 below all the other subcontractors' quotes. That could only mean one thing: This subcontractor had made a serious mistake.

George had two choices: He could use the erroneous quote as part of his own bid, which would give him a $30,000 edge on his competition. Of course, the project would end up with cost overruns, which would reflect poorly on his own company, and even more so on the subcontractor. Or, he could discard the low quote, inform the subcontractor of his mistake, and risk not getting the contract for the housing project. It was this second course that George chose. Fortunately, he got the job anyway.

Moreover, the subcontractor who filed the unrealistically low quote gave Robert George a hefty discount on a subsequent job, a tangible way of saying "thank you" for not taking advantage of his error.

Another businessman of integrity profiled in the same issue of *Nation's Business* was Jack Whiteman, CEO of Empire Southwest Corporation of Phoenix, Arizona. His company, which sells heavy earth-moving machinery, wanted to do business in Mexico. But many of the officials in that country demand bribes for the privilege of selling in their country's market. A lot of American companies just pay the customary *mordida* (meaning "a little bite") and chalk it up to the cost of doing business.

Jack Whiteman and Empire Southwest refused to pay. As a result, the Mexican market was closed to Whiteman's company throughout most of the 1960s. A lot of Whiteman's friends and competitors derided him as being naive and old-fashioned. "If you want to get ahead," they told him, "you have to be pragmatic. You have to play the game."

In 1967, however, Whiteman's ethical integrity paid off. The Mexican government approved the opening of two Empire Southwest dealerships. The reason: Whiteman's hard-line integrity had won the respect of government officials. They decided they wanted to do business with a company that would forego easy profits for the sake of principle and honesty.

The stories of Robert George and Jack Whiteman prove that integrity often pays, a lesson the American business community is just beginning to heed. As Ron Willingham wrote in *Integrity Selling:*

> The kind of person you are sends loud and clear signals to people. It communicates on the instinctive or intuitive level, but it communicates. . . . That is why integrity, honesty and genuine concern for your customers and their needs powerfully influence your ability to develop trust with people!
>
> When I get right down to it, who I am communicates! Sooner or later most people will get the message about the level of integrity I have. And they often get the message pretty quickly.[2]

Willingham's message is that *integrity pays*—and it's a welcome, refreshing message indeed. Yet if we are honest with ourselves, we have to acknowledge that while integrity often pays, it frequently *costs*.

THE COST OF INTEGRITY

In 1973, L. M. "Lem" Clymer was named president of Holiday Inns, Inc. During the decade of the 1970s, he was widely acclaimed as having restored prestige and profitability to the Holiday Inns hotel chain after it had suffered a period of decline. In 1977, while he was at the apex of his career with Holiday Inns, Clymer stunned the business world when he abruptly resigned his position. His reason: The board of directors had approved, over his objection, the construction of a $55 million hotel-casino in Atlantic City.

Only a few months after his resignation, my wife and I had dinner in Memphis with Lem and his wife. Over dinner, Clymer explained to us that his motivation for resigning was his love for Jesus Christ. "I had a vision of Holiday Inns," he said, "as a chain of family hotels. My desire for the company was that whenever people heard the name Holiday Inn, they would know it was a place where parents and kids could go for fun and relaxation, free of the sordid environment that always surrounds a casino. The board of Holiday Inns didn't share my vision and they voted for the casino."

"It must have been a hard decision," I said.

"Hard?" He seemed genuinely surprised by my comment, as if it had never occurred to him to make any decision other than the one he had made. "No, Ron, it wasn't hard at all. I knew what the Lord wanted me to do. It was all I *could* do. Not that I feel any resentment toward the board. They were just doing what they felt was best for the company and the shareholders. But I couldn't be a part of that decision. I couldn't do that and still maintain my own integrity."

There's no such thing in this world as cheap integrity. Integrity is absolute. And integrity has a price.

To have integrity is to be the same person you are alone, when no one is watching, as you are in the glare of the spotlight. As Howard Hendricks put it, "You show me a leader who is great in public and I will show you a leader who is even greater in private." That means that your secret inner self is seamlessly joined to your outer self. And that's very hard, isn't it? But to live any other way is to live a lie.

Our goal as mentors is to strive, in those moments of solitude when no one else can see, to exceed our public reputation as servants of Jesus Christ. As biblical mentors, we are called to live out our lives with total congruence between the way we live and what we say we believe. That's the only way to have an authentic and lasting effect on the lives of others.

"IT'S ALL IN THE LORD'S HANDS"

My brother Paul was a man of great integrity. In both the way he lived and the way he died, he demonstrated the power of a rock-solid inner and outer congruence to affect the lives of others, especially the life of his younger brother.

As a boy, Paul always stood out as a leader. He demonstrated an unswerving uprightness in the way he walked, even when confronted by peer pressure or temptation. I remember the night he came home from a party at a friend's house. He stopped by my room, and I could immediately tell he wasn't in a partying mood. "What's wrong?" I asked.

"I came home early," he said. "There was a lot of drinking going on. The guys tried to get me to drink, but I kept turning it down. Finally, they started laying in to me, calling me 'Preacher Boy' and worse. I wasn't having any fun, so I came home."

I knew it was tough for Paul to take a stand like that. I admired his strength. I wanted to be like him.

As a coach, Paul had the mentor's touch—the special quality of being able to see people not so much for what they are but for what they can become. He had a special ability to call forth the best effort and character qualities from the young men he coached. I believe this ability of Paul's accounts for the fact that, as coach of two Colorado high school basketball teams, he had the winningest percentage of any coach in the state.

During his final year of coaching, he led the Green Mountain High School Rams to the state championship. Then, to the surprise of many people, he retired. He wanted to spend more time with his wife and his two boys, who were moving into their adolescent years. Paul was a devoted husband to his wife, Jan, and father to his sons, Van and Shay; of all the people he mentored in all the arenas of his life, his family always came first. Even after he was diagnosed with cancer and was sick and weakened by the chemotherapy treatments, he would be in the bleachers at his sons' games, cheering and encouraging them on.

Even though he placed such a high priority on quality and quantity time with his family, Paul still gave countless hours to help kids with physical and mental disabilities. He also had a profound influence on scores of young athletes through his long association with the Fellowship of Christian Athletes. And he had a profound influence on me.

Paul was four years older than I, and I always looked up to him—when we were kids growing up in Iowa, when we were raising our respective families a thousand miles apart (he in Denver and I in California), and even as he faced cancer during the last days of his life. He only lived to be forty-one. But as Henri Nouwen once observed, the longevity of one's life does not matter nearly as much as the intensity with which it is lived. Paul lived his too-short span of life with intensity, with courage, with passion—but most of all, with integrity.

During the two months he lived after he was diagnosed with cancer of the liver, I talked with him on the phone every day. He always exuded a positive attitude, convinced he would beat the cancer. "It's all in the Lord's hands," he often said.

I was in Boise, Idaho, speaking at a pastors' conference with Ray Stedman, the week Paul was scheduled to go into surgery. It was supposed to be a fairly routine procedure involving the removal of some blood clots to keep them from moving into his lungs. Yet, within a few hours after this surgical procedure, Paul's battle with cancer would be ended.

During a break at the conference, I got a call from my nephew, Van. He was concerned about the surgery. "Dad's really sick," he said. "I really think you should be here when they do the surgery."

So I rearranged my schedule and flew to Denver, arriving the day before the surgery. "I didn't want you to break your schedule, Ron," said Paul when I came into his hospital room, "but I'm really glad you're here. You always give me a spiritual boost." Then he asked me question after question about the conference I had just come from. I was amazed that, with everything he was going through and all that he was facing, he was genuinely interested in me and in what I was doing.

And it wasn't just me. While I was there, he was visited by a number of young people he had coached. He took an individual interest in each person, chatting enthusiastically with each about his or her schoolwork, goals, and family life. I saw tears streaming unashamedly down the lean, tanned faces of these athletes in whom Paul had invested his life. I was profoundly struck by the fact that, no matter how great his own problems, Paul was always out of himself and into others, concerned about others, mentoring others.

That night, we talked about the surgery, about our years growing up together, and about life in general. He knew his condition was very serious. "Ron," he said, "with all the emotions I've experienced in these last few days, the one thing I haven't felt is fear. I thought I would be afraid to die, afraid of what the future holds, but I haven't been, not once. I've cried a lot, I've been sad about having to leave the people I love, but I haven't been afraid to die. I believe in Christ, and I believe in heaven, and I know, whatever happens, it's all in the Lord's hands."

Being so close to Paul, I knew he meant what he said. He was a big man physically, but not too big to cry, not too big to express how he really felt. And what he felt, even amid the sorrow and the loss, was a complete sense of calm and peace. I'm convinced that the source of this peace was the complete integrity and reality of his Christian faith. Throughout his life, he had walked his talk, and because of that reality, he could now walk unafraid into the valley of the shadow of death.

Early the next morning, Paul's wife, Jan, arrived, along with my mother, who had flown in the day before from Iowa. We spoke with Paul, sharing prayers, thoughts, and memories as the nurses prepared him for the surgery.

At eight o'clock, Jan and I hugged Paul, then gripped his hands as his gurney was wheeled down the corridor to surgery. We stopped at the door that led to the operating room, and I kissed Paul on the neck and told him I loved him. One last time, he said the words he had said so often in the past two months. "I love you, Ron. It's all in the Lord's hands."

Then Jan and Paul had a few precious moments together before he was wheeled out of our sight. The surgery did not go well. Unforeseen complications arose, and the procedure lasted four hours—longer than the doctors had expected. When Paul emerged, he was unable to breathe on his own, so he was placed on a respirator. He remained on the respirator the rest of that day and through the night.

The morning after the surgery, Paul began to have seizures. Between the seizures, he was conscious, but unable to speak. The doctors suggested to Jan that Paul be taken off the respirator. It was the hardest decision of her life, and she turned to me for advice. I placed some calls to several friends of mine in the medical profession and asked what it would mean, ethically and morally, to take Paul off the respirator. They all told me that it meant removing what is called "heroic means" of life support. Paul had once told us that he would rather be home with the Lord than left indefinitely on such life support. Moreover, Paul's doctors told us to expect his seizures to increase in severity and frequency.

"What should I do?" Jan asked me again.

I felt I already knew. But there was still one more person we needed to talk to. "Let's ask Paul," I said.

So Jan and I stood beside Paul's bed. His eyes were closed. He was very still. Jan bent close to Paul's ear and said, "Paul, dear, are you ready to go to be with God?" And Paul nodded firmly: *yes*. It was as if he was saying one last time, *It's all in the Lord's hands. I'm not afraid to die.*

Jan and I were with him immediately after the doctors removed the respirator. He was holding our hands, and I could feel his presence in those hands. Then that presence seemed to fade. He was drifting to sleep, drifting out of our lives. We felt him let go of our hands. Each breath came more faintly than the breath before. Finally, I couldn't feel him breathing at all. He was gone.

In the hours that followed, I thought often of his last words to me, and of the courage and peace he demonstrated in the last hours of his life. I thought of the way he nodded *yes* when Jan asked him if he was ready to go to be with God. I remembered the good times we shared growing up together in a little farming town in Iowa.

And I remembered one more thing: the day of my father's funeral. On that day, Paul had gone into different rooms around the house and taped up hand-lettered cards that read, "Character is not made in a crisis, it's only displayed there," the words of one of Paul's sports heroes, coach Vince Lombardi. Those words resonated in my mind after Paul's death. I had seen character displayed in the supreme crisis of my brother's life. I had seen faith and courage, hope and love. And I had seen great integrity, great consistency between the man Paul was on the outside and the man he was deep within.

When I spoke at Paul's funeral, I looked out at the sea of more than 1,200 faces. Among those 1,200 people were nearly 800 young men and women under the age of thirty whom Paul had either taught as a special education teacher or coached in the sport of basketball. Clearly, Paul had lived the life-style of a mentor. He had poured himself into the next generation. Again and again, in the days immediately following Paul's death, I heard people say things like: "You always knew where you stood with Paul." "He really lived the Christian life." "There was nothing phony or counterfeit about Paul Davis." "That guy was real."

In life and in death, my brother was a mentor to me. I want to have the inner and outer genuineness that marked his life.

I don't know how I will face my own death. But I know how I *want* to face it. I know because I've seen a man go through it without fear, but with integrity and with an unshakable faith in the faithfulness of God.

Chapter 7

DEVOTION

The prayer life of a mentor

DISSATISFIED CUSTOMERS

Dietrich Bonhoeffer was a godly man, a man of prayer. He opposed the evil of Hitlerism on German radio in 1933, even before Adolph Hitler came to power. He wrote several influential books on the Christian life, most notably his *Letters and Papers from Prison,* published after his execution in a Nazi concentration camp. He was a man who thought deeply, lived sacrificially, and spent countless hours of his life in prayer. Yet he once wrote, "My prayer life is something to be ashamed of."

I wonder why.

Martin Luther was the single most important figure in the Protestant Reformation. He is said to have spent a *minimum* of three hours in prayer every day. Yet when you study his writings, you find a man who was continually riddled with guilt and intensely dissatisfied with his prayer life.

Again, I have to wonder why.

If there were a Believers' Hall of Fame, it would be filled with Christian men and women who have expressed a deep dissatisfaction with their experience of prayer: St. Augustine, Thomas Aquinas, William Carey, Isaac Watts, Hudson Taylor,

Fanny Crosby, G. Campbell Morgan, Charles Haddon Spurgeon, Hannah Whitall Smith, Martin Lloyd Jones, F. B. Meyer, A. W. Tozer, Peter Marshall, and John R. W. Stott, to name a few. I wonder why there are so many dissatisfied customers when it comes to prayer.

What have we done to prayer to turn it into such an unapproachable ideal? Have we so raised our expectations about this activity called prayer that we have doomed ourselves to guilt, discouragement, and disappointment, no matter how much time we spend on our knees, no matter how fervently we engage in it? Have we turned prayer into such an elusive "holy grail" that even the most godly, faithful models and mentors of Christian history are made to feel like wretched failures?

I want to venture a partial answer to these questions. In so doing, I hope that we as mentors can learn to make prayer what it was meant to be in our lives, so that we can encourage and inspire our learners to be effective and persistent in their own prayer life.

I would submit to you that part of the reason there is such widespread dissatisfaction when it comes to prayer is that we have tried to make prayer fit into a mold it was never intended by God to fill. I submit that we have been victimized by misconceptions of what prayer should be. In setting such a high standard for prayer, we insure that we will never have peace about our prayer life, we will never quite feel we are "doing it right." Thus, we miss the very vitality, spontaneity, and genuineness that God planned for our prayer life.

THREE BARRIERS TO PRAYER

From my own life, from my mentors, and from my study of Scripture, I have found three basic barriers that tend to obstruct the prayer life of a mentor. These barriers sap the vitality of our prayers and hinder our effectiveness in the mentoring relationship. They are ritualism, repetition, and pride.[1]

Barrier #1: Ritualism

Jesus sternly preached against the deadly, formal ritualism that strangled the prayer life of the religious elite of his day. "Woe to you, scribes and Pharisees, hypocrites!" he exclaimed. "For you devour widows' houses, and for a pretense make long prayers. Therefore you will receive greater condemnation."[2]

The Jewish hierarchy of Jesus' time took the matter of prayer quite seriously. In fact, if you study the pages of history, you will not find any group of people more serious about prayer than the Jews of the first century A.D. And that was the problem. These Jewish leaders were so serious about prayer that the activity of talking to God had ceased to be a natural part of a relationship with God. Instead, it had become a religious rite. Gradually, a list of observances, laws, and rules grew up around prayer, and you had to follow these in just the right order in order to pray "correctly."

Prayers were standardized and memorized. Prayer was always conducted in a formal way, using a certain kind of flowery verbiage. Prayer was never spontaneous. Every part of the prayer had to be said in a certain order. There were sixteen adjectives—such as "sovereign," "eternal," "all-knowing," and so forth—that had to be expressed in a specified order before you could say the word *God*.

There was a certain position you were to assume when you prayed: standing, arms raised to heaven, palms out, eyes up. And every good Jew was to pray three times a day, at 9:00 A.M., noon, and 3:00 P.M. No matter where you were at those hours—whether in the temple, the marketplace, at home, or on the street corner—all business stopped so that you could perform the ritual of prayer.

Essentially, prayer had become a job for professionals, and those who could not perform the ritual in the right way—

ordinary merchants or farmers or fishermen—were made to feel inferior and separated from God.

We tend to feel sorry for those poor, bound-up, legalistic people of long ago, with all their silly rules and rituals. Yet I submit to you that in subtle (but in no less real) ways, religious ritualism is with us today. It is part of the prayer life of many sincere Christians. And it is a hindrance to the devotional life of a mentor.

When I was in seminary, one of my professors told me that whenever I prayed in public, I should have my prayer written out, line by line, sentence by sentence. The prayer should be grammatically correct and structured in a specified way. And if I was unable to prepare a written prayer in advance, then I should select a prayer from the *Book of Common Worship*. But by no means should I ever offer a prayer spontaneously in public, for the sentence structure might be wrong, or I might leave out a certain religious-sounding phrase.

This is no less ritualistic than the prayers the Pharisees prayed. Such prayers are more fitting to be offered to some stone idol than to a living, present God who is our Father and our Friend.

When I was in seminary, my friend Joe and I had a class together. It was taught by one of the most boring professors in the school. Like all of the classes in our school, this one always opened and closed with a word of prayer.

My friend Joe had a habit of dozing off during the hour-long lecture. This gave me an idea for a prank. Right in the middle of the lecture, after Joe had been asleep for about five minutes, I leaned over and nudged him. "Joe," I whispered, "class is over! The professor called on you to close in prayer!"

Joe leaped to his feet, startling not only the professor but the entire class, as he announced, "Fellow students, let us pray." Joe knew the ritual so well, he could go from a sound sleep to leading in prayer at the snap of a finger.

In our churches, our homes, and our mentoring relationships, we have prayer rituals too. We have routine and repetition and formality in our prayer life. Instead of communing and communicating with the living God of the universe, we "say our prayers" at mealtimes, at bedtimes, at meetings, at events. Let's not forsake prayer at these times, of course, but neither let us allow these to become mere dead rituals. Let's seek a living, daily relationship with Jesus Christ.

As mentors, we need to practice the continual presence of and fellowship with God. Whenever there is a joy, a triumph, an achievement to celebrate, let's not forget to celebrate it with God. Whenever there is a need, a sorrow, a failure, let's not forget to stop and seek God's guidance, comfort, and courage to go on. As mentors, let's show those within our sphere of influence that prayer is not a ritual to be performed, but an active dimension of a living relationship.

Barrier #2: Repetition

The Jews of the time of Christ performed their prayers in meaningless, repetitive liturgies. They were taught to offer to God a memorized prayer on a variety of different occasions: upon seeing a fire, upon seeing the new moon, upon entering or leaving a city, upon hearing good news or bad news. Such observances sound silly, until we realize that we do virtually the same thing today.

When I open my *Book of Common Worship* and glance down the table of contents, I find it is filled with prayers to be repeated, without heartfelt meaning, for any occasion. There is a printed prayer to be read whenever a church acquires a new piece of furniture. A prayer for the installation of a new church window. A prayer to dedicate a pulpit or lectern. The list goes on and on. Reading that list, I have to wonder: Where is the vitality of our prayer life?

I hesitate to make the next observation, because I know some people may be offended. Yet I feel a need to suggest that perhaps we do our children *no* favor when we teach them to pray, "God is great, God is good, and we thank Him for our food." Or, "Now I lay me down to sleep. I pray the Lord my soul to keep." Do we really want to convey to our children that God is a being to whom we recite repetitive lines of poetry, day after day, night after night? Or do we want our children to get to know God as an ever-present Friend?

And in our own prayer life as mentors, do we really carry on a dynamic conversation with God? Or do we simply recite our repertoire of canned phrases, our usual list of requests? Do we have our own version of "God is great, God is good"? Is it our ritual as adults to "say grace," to mutter, "Father, bless this food to the nourishment of our bodies and us to thy service, Amen"? Do we sprinkle our prayers with flowery phrases or spiritual-sounding verbiage?

Or do we treat our prayer life with the same kind of spontaneity, freshness, and energy that we treat, say, a phone call to a close and trusted friend? Does our prayer life accurately reflect the true state of our innermost being? Or is our prayer life just one more religious activity we engage in, one more spiritual pose we affect because that is what we think is expected of us?

When we, as mentors, pray with the learner, does that learner catch a glimpse of the human reality that throbs in the core of our being? What about when we are hurt and angry and disappointed with God? Are we afraid to reveal our true feelings, lest we disillusion the learner? Whose image are we protecting—God's or our own?

Reflecting on our mentoring relationship over the years, Barb Cummelin says, "Ron has always accepted me, with all my doubts and struggles. Whenever we talked or prayed together, he was always honest about his own hurts and that gave me permission to share my own struggles.

"Shortly after his brother died, Ron told me about his feeling angry with God. He was disappointed that God would let

Paul die at such a young age. Ron was showing me this human-ness during that stage of grief he was going through. That was a wonderful witness to me, because I've felt angry with God too.

"Some people are afraid that by expressing their own doubt and anger, they might damage someone else's faith or prayer life. But Ron's honesty helped me to pray more honestly and authentically."

"When you pray," said the Master Mentor, "do not use vain repetitions as the heathen do. For they think that they will be heard for their many words."[3] The vain repetition that is so deadly and stultifying to our prayer life must be replaced by the honest, natural reality of communing and communicating with God.

Barrier #3: Pride

The Jews of two thousand years ago prayed lengthy, ritualis-tic, repetitive prayers, and they looked down upon all those who did not. That was only natural and predictable, wasn't it? For whenever a man-made formula for "saying prayers" re-places an honest, sincere dialogue with God, then prayer be-comes a performance. And the motive behind performance is always pride.

Today, we ritualize and stylize prayer, filling our prayers with repetitive, hackneyed cliches. We burden others with our man-made formulas for prayer, saying, "You've got to have everything in just the right order. You have to begin with praise, then move to thanksgiving, then confession, then sup-plication, then petition, and you'd better do it in the right or-der." The result of our man-made formulas for prayer is the same as the result of those of the legalistic Jews of twenty cen-turies ago: the sin of spiritual pride.

Let me confess to you my own failure as a mentor in the area of prayer. I have frequently asked an intern, a staff member, an elder, a layperson, or a student to lead in public prayer and afterward have leaned over and whispered to that person,

"That was a beautiful prayer." I have affirmed the *performance* of prayer. I have encouraged spiritual pride. As if what really matters is that a prayer be beautifully performed, with high-sounding words, with impressive arrangement, with pleasing tone. Subtly, whether consciously or not, I have communicated that what matters in a prayer is that it be said "correctly," "beautifully," and—tragically!—with pride.

The goal of prayer is a vital relationship with God. Any other motive blunts the effectiveness of prayer. And the motive of pride can even turn prayer into a sin.

"DADDY, CAN YOU HELP ME?"

There is an interesting paradox about prayer that illustrates how overwhelmingly *mutual* the mentoring process is. That paradox is this: There are two kinds of people who have more to teach us about prayer than anyone else. Contrary to what we might expect, these two kinds of people are not the sort we normally think of as having much to teach us. They are not seminary professors or great Christian authors or leading pastors. The people who have the most to teach you and me about prayer are *children* and *new Christians*.

In the mid-1970s, when I was chaplain for the Minnesota Vikings and Howard Hendricks was chaplain for the Dallas Cowboys, I attended a conference where Hendricks told the story of Tom, a young Cowboys player who had just turned his life over to Christ. Throughout the twenty-odd years of Tom's life, he had never once set foot inside a church. He didn't know any of the Christian jargon that many of us older Christians freely sprinkle in our prayers.

Soon after his conversion, Tom attended a Bible study with some other Christian teammates, led by Howard Hendricks. At the end of the Bible study, everyone stood and bowed their heads. Tom looked around the circle of men, not sure what was happening. One by one, Tom's teammates began to pray.

"Dear Heavenly Father . . ." started one. After he finished, the next in line began, "Oh, Lord . . ." Next, "Dear God . . ." One by one, they prayed, some speaking in King James Thees and Thous, some speaking in language Tom understood. With a sudden sense of dread, Tom realized that the spotlight was moving around the circle *toward him,* and he had *never* prayed out loud in his life!

When his turn came, Tom said, "Hi, God. This is Tom. Remember me? I met you last week and I asked you to live in my heart. It was at my house—you know, at the corner of Elm and Mesa Drive?" Hendricks said he was waiting for Tom to tell God his zip code. "You know, God," Tom continued, "it's been a really hard week. I mean, I never thought it would be so hard being a Christian. But, well, my wife doesn't understand. She keeps calling me a religious fanatic. And some of the guys on the team have been calling me 'Jesus freak.' I don't know what to say to them, and God, I really need your help."

That's authentic prayer.

We tend to think that children and new Christians haven't yet learned how to pray "properly." But the more I listen to their prayers, the more I'm convinced that they have something the rest of us more "mature" Christians have largely lost. They have a vitality and a genuineness in their prayer life, because they have not yet been indoctrinated by the false pressures of our religious culture. Whereas many more "mature" Christians *perform* prayer, children and new Christians simply talk to God. They instinctively know what the Scriptures exhort us to remember: that the One who created the universe is also the One we go to and say, "Abba, Father!"

That's the way Jesus addressed his Father as he prayed in the garden, just hours before the Cross: "Abba, Father, all things are possible for You. Take this cup away from Me; nevertheless, not what I will, but what You will."[4]

Because Jesus obediently drank of that cup and died on the

cross, Paul said we now have the same access to the Father that Jesus had. Now we, too, can pray, "Abba, Father." "You received the Spirit of adoption by whom we cry out 'Abba, Father,'" Paul wrote. "And because you are sons, God has sent forth the Spirit of His Son into your hearts, crying out, 'Abba, Father!'"[5]

That word *abba* is an Aramaic term that is best rendered in English, "Daddy," or even, "Da-da." Like the affectionate cooing of a toddler who is just learning to talk to his father, it's an expression of love, trust, and helplessness. How much more sincere and genuine it is to come before God as a toddler approaches his daddy than to rattle off a string of adjectives such as "O most holy, most gracious, most wise and omniscient . . ."

I think of the times my son Nathan or my daughter Rachael comes to me with a problem having to do with schoolwork or a difficulty with a friend or some possession that needs to be mended. If you're a parent, then you know what it means to hear that knock on the door and the child's voice pleading, "Daddy, can you help me?" That's what a child's prayer is like. That's what *real* prayer is like.

"Daddy, can you help me?" I'm reminded of these childlike words so often when I'm dealing with a difficult situation in my counseling room, or when I'm speaking before a group and I lose my train of thought and don't know what to say next, or when I'm in a business meeting wrestling with a difficult issue, or when I'm grieving over a loss or a disappointment in life. A plea goes straight from my heart to God's heart: "Daddy, can you help me?" That's a biblical prayer. That's honest, live, unscripted, unrehearsed communication with God. That's the kind of prayer we need to practice in our mentoring relationships.

Study the Bible carefully, and I am convinced you will not find a single admonition to pray beautifully, pray eloquently, pray in grandiose words. Not one.

And I can't think of anything that would do more harm to the prayer life of your learner than to somehow communicate that there is a "right way" and a "wrong way" to pray. I can't think of anything more damaging than to teach the learner that prayer is a matter of form and structure and style rather than a matter of honest feelings. For if that is what you convey, the learner is likely to conclude, "I'll never be able to pray that way. I'm just no good at praying." And that would spell a tragic reversal of the mentoring process.

Most of what I have learned about prayer has not come from books. It has not come from sermons I've heard. It has not come from anyone telling me I need to pray or teaching me techniques for prayer. Most of what I have learned about prayer has come from my mentors. My life has been a school of prayer taught by many teachers. And they didn't teach me so much by their words as by their lives.

THE PRIORITY OF PRAYER

As mentors, you and I are teaching by our lives. Every day, we are making a statement about the value and priority we place on contact with God. Does the way we live our lives communicate to those about us that we genuinely *cherish* a vital, constant, intimate link with God?

I have mentioned Henry Chin several times already. Henry is a man who places great priority on prayer. He was a member of the search committee that called me to my first senior pastorate in California. And over the years, I have gotten to know Henry very well and to love him deeply as a brother in Christ.

He told Jim Denney, my co-author, about the place of prayer in our mentoring relationship. "Ron worked hard to build a relationship with each elder," he said. "The elders met for study, fellowship, and prayer every Sunday morning. Several, including myself, were unable to attend on Sunday mornings (I was busy with the Inquirers' Class), so Ron set aside an additional time of prayer on Wednesday evenings. I always came every Wednesday after work.

"In the beginning there were three or four of us, but it eventually dwindled down to just Ron and me. Yet Ron never asked to discontinue that time. He kept meeting and praying with me alone. I never told him before, but it meant a lot to me that he maintained that prayer time with me, as precious as his time was. It said a lot to me about the priority Ron places on prayer."

I never told Henry before, either, but it meant a lot to me that he was so faithful in keeping that prayer time with me. It says to me that Henry is also a man who believes in the priority of prayer.

MY PRAYER MENTORS

By far, the mentors who have taught me the most about prayer have been my father and mother.

When I was a boy, we lived in a parsonage across the street from the church. Most evenings, my mother would send me across the street to call my father for dinner. I always went first to his office, then, if he wasn't in his office, I went to the sanctuary. I remember many times peeking into the sanctuary from the rear door. It was dark inside, but I could just see the silhouette of my dad in one of the front pews, head bowed, deep in prayer.

At my dad's funeral, many people stood and told of the wonderful things he did, the tremendous Christian character he had, the love and compassion he showed to everyone around him. But I saw what none of those people ever saw: the bowed silhouette in the darkened sanctuary. That was the source of all the wonderful things people saw in my dad's life: hours and hours spent in a solitary place with God.

Another vivid memory from my boyhood is one of coming home after school and running upstairs to my bedroom to get some baseball cards or my basketball. On the way, I would pass the master bedroom, and if the door was open a crack, I would see my mother on her knees. After she finished praying, she would come down and put dinner on the table. There was always a tangible spirit of love and grace in her manner after those prayer times. I must have witnessed that scene scores of times, but she never knew it.

To this day, my mother continues to challenge and inspire my prayer life with her own consistency in prayer. Every winter, she comes from Iowa and spends a few months in our California home. During her most recent visit, I went past her room and saw that she was on her knees, praying, just as I remember seeing her do so many times when I was a boy.

Clearly, prayer was not just a part of my parents' lives, but the center of their lives. That's how I learned about prayer. It wasn't their words. It was the way they lived, the quality of their lives.

From my mentors, I have learned that the Creator of the Universe has given us access to him. He allows us to freely call on him, saying, "Abba! Father! Daddy! Can you help me?" What an amazing, transforming truth. And this is the truth which must be reflected in the devotional life of every biblical mentor.

Chapter 8

WISDOM
A mentor at the crossroads

CHRISTIAN NON-CONFORMISTS

A few years ago, a test was conducted among hundreds of high school and college students. In this experiment, ten students were placed in a room together. The group was shown a series of cards, each card featuring two lines—some parallel to each other, some perpendicular, some at oblique angles. The group was to vote on which of the two lines on each card was longer. However, only one of the ten people in the group was an actual test subject. The other nine had been instructed ahead of time to choose the shorter line. That is, they were instructed to lie.

During the test, all the unwitting test subjects began by raising their hands and correctly choosing the longer line. But they began noticing after the first couple of cards that the other nine people in the room always chose the *shorter* line. No one else in the room agreed with the test subjects' choice. Soon, the test subjects began to hesitate, waiting to see which line the rest of the group chose. Then they would raise their hands and agree with the majority.

The result of the test was that roughly three-fourths of all the test subjects yielded to the pressure to conform. Only a quarter stood by their own convictions. Even though the difference between the two lines was unmistakable, most people chose to believe as the group did rather than to believe the evidence of their own eyes.

The lesson for you and me as mentors is that most of the people in this world are willing to go along with the majority. Most people are very susceptible to the pressure of society. So in our mentoring, we had better prepare our learners to stand up for what they believe, to stand completely alone if need be, to make godly decisions, and to exercise wisdom.

As Christians, our vision is not the world's vision. Our priorities and values are not the priorities and values of the world. We are called by God to be Christian non-conformists, at odds with the world and the surrounding culture.

We are in a battle against the systems of this world, of which Satan is the prince. In this battle, being piously religious just isn't enough. God calls us to exchange our sugar and spice for salt and light. It was the existentialist philosopher Camus who challenged the church with these words: "We stand in need of Christians who shall plant themselves squarely in the bloody face of history and make a difference." The world needs courageous Christians who have the *wisdom* to make tough, lonely, morally right choices.

WISDOM IN AN AGE OF PROSPERITY

Life is about making choices. And *wisdom,* as I would define it, is the combined judgment and courage to make *right* choices, even when pressured to do wrong. Wisdom is a kind of spiritual and ethical compass, an inner sense of direction that enables us, when we come to a crossroads, to choose the right way.

It might seem that it has become easier to make choices in life as a result of our increasing affluence. In fact, the opposite is true. As Thomas Carlyle once observed, "Adversity is hard on a man, but for one man who can stand prosperity there are a hundred who can stand adversity."

Do those words sound strange to you? Some people might argue, "What does that mean, Ron? Prosperity is a blessing, adversity is a trial! I can always stand a bit more prosperity in my life!"

But as I have watched the lives of people who have been given great prosperity, I can tell you that Carlyle's words ring true. In the arena of integrity, of honesty, of humility, of maintaining one's moral and spiritual equilibrium, prosperity can be very hard on a man or a woman.

Carlyle's words remind me of a professional football player I became acquainted with when I was the Bible teacher for the Minnesota Vikings in the mid-1970s. During his rookie year with the Vikings, this player stood in the pulpit of our church in Minneapolis and gave a thrilling, powerful testimony of his faith in Jesus Christ. He said that Jesus Christ was the only thing that really mattered in his life.

In the years that followed, this man's fame and prosperity grew. And as his prosperity grew, his testimony diminished. He drifted away from his faith in Jesus Christ. He defected both spiritually and morally. Not long ago, he told a friend of mine that all that really matters to him these days is accumulating wealth.

I've seen the same scenario played out in many other lives—in those of professional athletes, successful businessmen, and even well-known Christian leaders. Adversity is hard for any of us to withstand. But all too often, prosperity is even harder. Why? Because it takes a lot of *wisdom* to withstand the seduction of prosperity. It takes a lot of *wisdom* to live in the lap of luxury and still keep a righteous moral, spiritual, and ethical perspective.

You may be thinking, "Well, prosperity is not a problem with me. I'm just struggling along, trying to pay my bills like everybody else. I'm certainly not what anyone would call 'rich.'"

Really?

I have had the privilege of traveling to many parts of the world, including Korea, Singapore, Eastern Europe, and Africa. I see what the people in those places struggle with: hunger, poverty, government oppression and persecution, and much more. Then I come back to this massive concentration of wealth, plenty, luxury, and entertainment we call America and I think, "Even the most ordinary citizen of this land is a virtual king compared with most of the people in the places I've visited. We are *rich!*"

We live in a country where over 70 percent of all households own VCRs. There is roughly one automobile for every man, woman, and child in the United States. If California alone were an independent country, it would be the seventh richest country in the world—and that's just one state out of fifty. In America, we have every kind of convenience, contrivance, technological wonder, and entertainment medium known in the history of civilization. If we are not rich, who is?

In the midst of our prosperity, a wise man or a wise woman will consider the words of Psalm 75:6–7:

> *For exaltation comes neither from the east*
> *Nor from the west nor from the south.*
> *But God is the Judge:*
> *He puts down one,*
> *And exalts another.*

Prosperity does not come by luck or by being in the right place at the right time or by knowing the right people. It comes by God's grace. Even though wealth almost always comes as a consequence of hard work, planning, and diligence, it is still God who gave us the intelligence, the good health, and endurance to do the work. A biblical mentor understands this truth, lives by it, and solemnly teaches it to his learner. Without an understanding of this truth, it is impossible for us to maintain a wise equilibrium amid prosperity.

Search the Scriptures and you will find many examples of people who were dragged down, morally and spiritually, by their wealth, prestige, and privilege: King Saul, who went mad with paranoia, fearing the loss of his power. The wicked kings of Judah, such as Rehoboam, Abijah, Jehoram, and Jehoiakim. David, who sinned when he committed adultery with Bathsheba and used the power of his throne to have Bathsheba's husband killed. The rich young ruler of Luke 18, who could not follow Christ because he clutched his wealth. Ananias and Sapphira, wealthy donors who gave to the church out of hypocritical motives.

We have to conclude that very few men and women of Scripture were able to respond to prosperity from a wise perspective. Most of them stumbled. No wonder, then, that Jesus said, "It is easier for a camel to go through the eye of a needle than for a rich man to enter the kingdom of God."[1] He was not saying that wealth is a sin. He was saying that wealth is a snare, and only the wise can resist its lure.

Those few people in the Bible who were able to maintain their faith, obedience, and integrity amid prosperity were also people of extraordinary wisdom. Take, for example, Joseph.

The book of Genesis tells how, after being sold into slavery and falsely imprisoned, Joseph ultimately ascended to the position of prime minister of all Egypt. Despite his power and wealth, he never gave in to arrogance or selfishness. At every crucial juncture of his life, he responded with wisdom: He wisely resisted the advances of the wife of his employer, Potiphar; he impressed Pharaoh with the wisdom of his food allocation plan for the nation of Egypt; he wisely resisted the temptation to use his enormous political power to take revenge against the brothers who sold him into slavery. Joseph, a man of wealth and power, was also a man of godly wisdom.

Another man of godly wisdom was Daniel. A handsome,

brilliant man of royal blood and great fame, as well as a trusted advisor to the king of Babylon, Daniel was also a wise and upright servant of God. He understood that the source of wealth, power, and wisdom was God alone. He said:

> *Blessed be the name of God forever and ever*
> *For wisdom and might are His. . . .*
> *He removes kings and raises up kings;*
> *He gives wisdom to the wise*
> *And knowledge to those who have understanding.*[2]

The test of Daniel's wisdom was the decree by King Darius that everyone should worship Darius alone, and should not pray to any other god or man. Daniel, then a governor, second in power only to King Darius himself, was presented with a very simple, clear-cut choice: Obey the king and continue to enjoy the luxury and power to which he had become accustomed or obey God and be executed. But wealth and power did not blind Daniel to his true allegiance. He made the choice to worship God and was arrested, tried, sentenced, and thrown to the lions. But the Lord spared Daniel's life. Daniel wisely understood who raised kings, who removed kings, and who gave wisdom.

Both Joseph and Daniel possessed *wisdom, the uncommon ability to make righteous decisions under enormous pressure*. Even though surrounded by the lure of prosperity, they chose the right direction when standing at the crossroads of decision.

THE ETHICS CHECK

I know of one Christian leader who travels around the country. In his travels he is often alone and is virtually answerable to no one. He can do exactly as he pleases, for no one is watching him. There is great moral peril in such freedom.

Being keenly aware of the peril of his freedom, this man

keeps a journal under lock and key. In the back of this journal he has listed the names and circumstances of friends of his who have stumbled while in the lap of luxury, privilege, and prosperity. Not long ago, he wrote these words: "This morning, I entered name number 42. It was a case of a Christian leader who willfully misappropriated ministry funds for his own use. He has just been found guilty of grand theft."

This world is in desperate need of people who have the wisdom to make righteous, ethical choices in their most public actions and in their most private moments. This world needs wise mentors.

Where, then, does wisdom come from? How can we as mentors learn to choose the right way when we come to a crossroads of decision?

It may sound simplistic—the most profoundly true answers often do—but the two sources of wisdom are the Word of God and prayer. "The testimony of the LORD is sure," observed the psalmist, "making wise the simple."[3] "If any of you lacks wisdom," wrote James, "let him ask of God, who gives to all liberally and without reproach, and it will be given to him."[4]

With prayer and the Bible, we prepare and prime our minds with the values, beliefs, and mode of thinking of a biblical mentor. Then, when we find ourselves suddenly at a crossroads, our minds are so steeped in the thinking of God, so attuned to the mind of Christ, that we automatically respond in the way he would respond.

In their book *The Power of Ethical Management*, Kenneth Blanchard and Norman Vincent Peale offer a three-question quiz which enables us to inspect all our decisions through the lens of wisdom and ethical integrity. They call their test The Ethics Check. And though they devised The Ethics Check as a guide for business decisions, I have expanded it to make it relevant to such arenas as churches and organizations. The three questions of the The Ethics Check are:

1. Is It Legal?

Will the decision or action I make be legal, not only according to the criminal and civil code of the government, but according to the rules and policies of the company, the club, the organization, or the church which is affected by this decision? This question forces you to examine the decision or action in light of standards that are in place within the surrounding society.

2. Is It Balanced?

In other words, is this decision or action fair and balanced toward all parties, or is there a winner and a loser? Does this decision promote a "win-win" relationship? This question forces you to examine the decision or action in light of your sense of fairness and justice.

3. How Will It Make Me Feel About Myself?

If my decision or action were to be published in the national press, would I feel gratified or ashamed? Would I feel good if my parents, wife, or children knew about it? This question forces you to examine the decision in light of your own feelings, values, and conscience.If the decision or action you are contemplating fails *any one* of these tests, it has failed the entire test. Wisdom says, "No, don't do it."[5]

THE FIVE E'S TEST

There is another test I have found useful for decision-making in those "gray areas" of life, where no clear-cut guidance from Scripture can be found. I call it The Five E's Test, and it consists of questions in five categories: Emulation, Excess, Evangelism, Edification, and Example.

1. Emulation

Will this decision or activity help me to emulate Christ? Will it help me to walk in the footsteps of the Master Mentor? In

1 John 2:6 John says, "He who says he abides in [Jesus] ought himself also to walk just as He walked." I may feel I have perfect freedom to engage in an activity the Bible does not clearly prohibit; yet I should first ask myself, Will engaging in this activity help me as I seek to emulate Christ and walk as he would walk? If not, this activity fails the test.

2. *Excess*

Will this decision or activity just add more excess to an already overcrowded life? Do I need this activity in my life, or will it hinder me in my goal of becoming more like Jesus Christ?

When I was running the half-mile in college, my favorite verse was Hebrews 12:1: "Therefore we also, since we are surrounded by so great a cloud of witnesses, let us lay aside every weight, and the sin which so easily ensnares us, and let us run with endurance the race that is set before us." In light of this verse, the question of excess is crucial: Will this activity weigh me down and ensnare me as I seek to run the race of the Christian life? If the answer is yes, this activity fails the test.

3. *Evangelism*

If I'm involved in this activity, is my witness to the world going to be enhanced or diminished?

Tucked away in the book of Colossians is a strategically important verse that speaks volumes regarding the relationship between wisdom, decision-making, and evangelism. It says, "Walk in wisdom toward those who are outside, redeeming the time."[6] That means that as you go through your life, as you are being watched by "those who are outside" (meaning outside the Christian faith), you are to make sure that your walk, your behavior, your actions, and your decisions reflect credit and honor to your faith.

You are to walk wisely in the way you treat your employees, your colleagues, your neighbors, your customers, and the people in the businesses you patronize, because all of these people are watching you. You are to walk wisely, even when conflicts and disagreements arise. All the scores of people within your sphere of influence are learning about the Christian faith from you. They are deciding to move either toward or away from Jesus Christ, based on the evidence of your life.

In light of the issue of evangelism, the question we must ask ourselves at any moral crossroads is, Will this activity help or hinder my witness to others?

4. Edification

Will this activity edify me? The word *edify* comes from a root word which means "to build up." That's why a building is sometimes called an edifice.

So the question is, Will this activity build me up? The apostle Paul put it this way: "All things are lawful for me, but not all things are helpful; all things are lawful for me, but not all things edify."[7] Paul was telling us that we have enormous freedom in Christ. But a lot of things you are free to do will not build you up. In fact, some will tear you down.

So this is another test to which we must wisely submit our decisions in the gray areas of life: Will this activity edify me?

5. Example

Would my involvement in this activity be a good example to my Christian brother or sister? "It is good," said Paul, "neither to eat meat nor drink wine nor do anything by which your brother stumbles or is offended or is made weak."[8] This is really an extension of the "Edification" test to others beyond ourselves: Will this activity edify my Christian brothers? Will it build them up or tear them down?

The principle implicit in the "Example" test is embodied in this simple phrase: *Love limits liberty*. There are many things we are free to do as Christians, but wisdom dictates that we not do some of these things if we truly love our Christian brothers and sisters.

I've been in settings where Christians who consider themselves very wise and liberated gather with glasses of wine or mixed drinks in their hands, while poking fun at those poor uptight, legalistic Christians who don't realize they have the liberty to drink. To tell you the truth, I'm very tired of witnessing that kind of smug, superior "Christian liberty" in action. I'm very tired of that judgmental attitude which says, "I've matured beyond the legalistic phase in my own Christian wisdom."

One reason I am so weary of that sort of "Christian liberty" is I've known people like my friend Jerry, who used to be one of those who made jokes about his abstaining Christian brothers and sisters. Jerry doesn't joke about them anymore. Not long ago, I visited Jerry in the chemical dependence treatment unit of a hospital. Jerry used to think he was so wise and so liberated. When I visited him, he told me, "I've been such a fool. I feel so trapped."

A wise mentor considers the example he sets for those who are watching his life, and he remembers the sober counsel of Paul, "Let no one seek his own, but each one the other's well-being."[9]

AT THE CROSSROADS

A recent survey of high school students confronts us with some devastating information regarding the ability of the next generation to make wise choices. First, this survey found that 75 percent of all high school students regularly cheat in their schoolwork and feel it is all right to do so. Second, this survey found that 30 percent of all high school seniors had shoplifted within the past thirty days. Third, 50 percent of all teenage pregnancies end in abortion. Fourth, one out of every nine teenagers is an alcoholic. Fifth, 1,100 teenagers attempt suicide every day. Sixth, one-tenth of all high school students actively engage in a homosexual life-style. Seventh—and perhaps the most shocking—65 percent of all high school students *who describe themselves as Christians* are sexually active.

In an age when most of the people in this world are willing to go along with the majority, the task of biblical mentors is to build into the next generation the ability to think clearly, decide wisely, and take hard, lonely stands for what is right and godly. The world needs mentors who can stand at the crossroads and not only choose the right way, but point out the right way to others.

Chapter 9

MOTIVATION
Energizing others for service

"HE WAS MY MENTOR—AND MY *TOR*MENTOR!"

You've probably never heard of Charlie Beacham. A Southern gentleman with a keen mind and a genial personality, Beacham worked for the Ford Motor Company as its eastern regional manager in Chester, Pennsylvania. Beacham was also a mentor to a young Ford salesman named Lido.

Lido was the son of poor Italian immigrant parents. He had been hired to work in fleet sales at the Chester office, and he was struggling in the job. One day, Beacham noticed Lido walking dejectedly through the garage. "Hey, Lido," he said, throwing one arm around the young man's shoulders, "what are you so down about?"

"Mr. Beacham," the salesman replied, "you've got thirteen salesmen selling in thirteen zones, and you're looking at the guy who finished number thirteen in sales this month."

"C'mon, kid!" said Beacham. "Don't let that get you down! Somebody's gotta be last!" He slapped the young man on the back and walked toward his own car. As he opened the car door, he turned and called out to Lido, "But listen! Just don't you be last two months in a row, hear?"

As a mentor, Charlie Beacham was tough but fair. He gave young Lido advice, showed him the ropes of the business, and most important, instructed him in the kind of character needed for success in business and in life.

"Always remember," Beacham once told him, "everyone makes mistakes. Trouble is, most people won't own up to their mistakes. Some guys blame their mistakes on the weather, on their wives, on their kids, on their dogs—never on themselves. If you foul up around here, I want you to come to me and own up to it, no excuses, no alibis."

Charlie Beacham gradually gave Lido more and more responsibility. He assigned him to teach local dealers how to sell trucks. He let the young man produce a sales handbook for the company. He sent Lido on sales and training trips up and down the eastern seaboard.

Lido didn't just learn about the car business from Charlie Beacham. He learned about life, about perseverance, about decision-making, about personal responsibility. Charlie Beacham, Lido later recalled, had "more impact on my life than any person other than my father. . . . He was a great motivator—the kind of guy you'd charge up the hill for, even though you knew very well you could get killed in the process. He had the rare gift of being tough and generous at the same time. . . . He was not only my mentor, he was more than that. He was my *tor*mentor. But I love him!"[1] Lido took the knowledge, skills, character, and maturity he acquired under the mentorship of Charlie Beacham and put it to good use throughout his career at Ford, and later at the Chrysler Corporation.

The ultimate test of his skill and character came in the early 1980s when, as Chrysler's chief executive officer, he led the company from the brink of disaster ($4.75 billion in debt in 1980) to stratospheric heights of success ($925 million in the black in 1983). Today, as you've already guessed, Lido is better known as Lee Iacocca. Auto industry analysts attribute the amazing turnaround of the Chrysler Corporation to this one man.

Iacocca, in turn, gives much of the credit for the shaping of his own values and character to his mentor, Charlie Beacham.

"Character," as Vince Lombardi said, "is not made in a crisis. It's only displayed there." I submit to you that the character of Lee Iacocca was made not in the Chrysler financial crisis but, in large part, in the mentoring relationship between Charlie Beacham and a young car salesman named Lido.

The words Iacocca used to describe Charlie Beacham would be a worthy epitaph for any biblical mentor: "*He was a great motivator*—the kind of guy you'd charge up the hill for even though you knew very well you could get killed in the process." In truth, one of the primary tasks of a mentor is to motivate the learner, to energize him or her for sacrifice and service to God and to others.

ORDINARY PEOPLE, EXTRAORDINARY MOTIVATION

An admirer once told Teddy Roosevelt, "Mr. Roosevelt, you are a great man!"

Roosevelt brushed the compliment aside. "Oh, no, I'm not a great man. I'm just an ordinary man who is greatly motivated for the cause of my country."

Our job as mentors is not to produce great men and women, but rather to energize ordinary men and women to be greatly motivated for the cause of Jesus Christ.

The Old Testament prophet Nehemiah was a man who energized others for service. He was not only greatly motivated himself, but a great motivator of others. Nehemiah left the royal city of Susa, where he was a high official in the government of King Artaxerxes, and he went to Jerusalem with the goal of rebuilding the shattered walls of the city. He took a dispirited and discouraged group of people who had just been released from foreign exile, and he molded and motivated them into a disciplined, cohesive force for rebuilding. How did he do it?

1. Nehemiah Was Bold.

Nehemiah wasn't afraid to take risks. He didn't hesitate to attack difficult tasks. Some scoffed, telling him that the job was impossible. But Nehemiah boldly dared to dream great dreams and to make those dreams come true. Alan Kay of Apple Computers once said, "The best way to predict the future is to make it happen." Nehemiah was the kind of bold visionary who made things happen.

2. Nehemiah Was a Planner.

Nehemiah understood that boldness without careful planning is just recklessness. When he first arrived in Jerusalem, he could have immediately rolled up his sleeves, requisitioned some bricks, and started barking orders. But that was not Nehemiah's way. Instead, he took three days and did nothing but walk around the city, inspect the gates, examine the ruins, pray, and plan his task. Nehemiah intuitively grasped this principle stated by Howard Hendricks: "I am convinced that any leader who does not spend at least fifteen percent of his time in thinking is systematically setting himself up for failure."

A noted surgeon once said, "If I knew I only had five minutes to perform a delicate operation, I would spend the first two minutes planning the procedure." A mentor who motivates others is a mentor who thinks and plans.

3. Nehemiah Articulated and Shared His Vision.

"You see the distress that we are in,'" he told the people, "how Jerusalem lies waste, and its gates are burned with fire. Come and let us build the wall of Jerusalem, that we may no longer be a reproach."[2] He was open about his intentions, and he included the people in his counsel.

4. Nehemiah Identified with the People.

Notice that he said, "You see the distress that *we* are in. . . . Come and let *us* build . . . that *we* may no longer be a reproach." Nehemiah did not inspire the troops from an ivory tower but from down in the trenches.

Some leaders and mentors might say, "I'm the boss and here's the plan. If you have any problems or questions, come see me in my office." Not Nehemiah. He involved himself with his people. He rolled up his sleeves and labored alongside them.

5. Nehemiah Challenged the People.

He didn't coddle them or sugar coat the situation. Instead, he issued a tough challenge. He said, in effect, "Look, the city is in ruins, the gates are burned, and we're in disgrace. But we're not going to let that stop us. Now, let's get out there and build!"

Notice that Nehemiah did not motivate the people by saying, "If you help me rebuild the wall, there'll be something in it for you. Those who work the hardest will get a bonus, a nice home, a high-paying job." Nehemiah used a mentor's approach to motivating his people. He intuitively understood the difference between the two basic kinds of motivation: *extrinsic* and *intrinsic*.

EXTRINSIC MOTIVATION

Extrinsic motivation is motivation from without. Extrinsic motivation involves the inducement of behavior with rewards. If you give your child money for getting good grades, that's extrinsic motivation. If your employer offers you a bonus for achieving a certain level of sales or productivity, that's extrinsic motivation. When my friend Jeff Siemon, former linebacker for the Minnesota Vikings, led the team in tackles and received extra pay according to the incentive clause in his contract, he was given extrinsic motivation.

There is nothing inherently wrong with extrinsic motivation. It has long been an effective means of inspiring people to work harder, be more productive, and perform with greater excellence. Even in a mentoring relationship, I believe in rewarding behavior when it's appropriate. However, extrinsic motivation is generally less effective over the long term than intrinsic motivation.

INTRINSIC MOTIVATION

Intrinsic motivation is motivation that comes from within. Intrinsic motivation calls forth our innermost resources, values, and beliefs in order to energize our behavior. A biblical mentor learns to appeal to the intrinsic, inner motivations of the learner, often inspiring behavior that is completely at odds with the extrinsic, outer dynamics of the situation.

This means that the intrinsically motivated person is often inspired to attempt a task precisely because that task is difficult, stressful, painful, or personally costly. Notice that when Nehemiah motivated his people to rebuild the wall around Jerusalem, he didn't say, "We're going to make a fun little spare-time project out of this. If the weather gets a little too hot, we'll knock off early. If anybody gets tired, well, there are the lemonade stand and the shade trees. Donate an hour, two hours, whatever you can spare. Jerusalem's going to be here a long time, and with your help, we'll get this wall rebuilt eventually."

No, Nehemiah gave a tough challenge, a demanding challenge. "You see the distress that we are in," he says. "Come and let us build the wall of Jerusalem, that we may no longer be a reproach." There is urgency and insistence in his call.

Nehemiah motivated his followers in much the same way Winston Churchill intrinsically motivated the people of Great Britain to dedicate themselves to the war effort during the darkest days of World War II.

I have nothing to offer you but blood, sweat, and tears [not a very motiviational beginning, is it?]. Victory at all cost, victory instead of terror, victory however long and hard the road may be; for without victory there is no survival.

We shall not flag or fail. We shall go on to the end. We shall fight in France, we shall fight in the seas and oceans, we shall fight with growing confidence and growing strength in the air; we shall defend our island whatever the cost may be and we shall never surrender.

Death and sorrow will be the companions of our journey, hardship our garment, constancy and valor our only shield. We must be united! We must be undaunted! We must never give up!

This is a tough, demanding call to commitment and sacrifice. This is an appeal to the people's intrinsic motivation, the same kind of motivation Jesus appeals to when he tells his disciples, "If anyone desires to come after Me, let him deny himself, and take up his cross, and follow Me. For whoever desires to save his life will lose it, but whoever loses his life for My sake will find it."[3]

A biblical, Christlike mentor is one who has learned to motivate intrinsically.

One of the best ways I know to motivate intrinsically is to *invest trust* in people. In my own mentoring relationships, I try to give the learner a task, let him deal with it on his own, without looking over his shoulder or criticizing or taking it over. That sometimes means tasks don't always get performed exactly as I might perform them myself. But we must always remember that growth, not the completion of a task, is the goal of mentoring. Our objective is to build character and confidence, and to do that, we must treat the learner as a colleague, not as a rookie.

Reflecting on our relationship, Joe Pettit recalls, "My friendship with Ron didn't feel like a teacher-student relationship so much as it felt like the adventure of two sojourners—one with more experience, more expertise. Ron was the senior pastor, I was the associate, but Ron engendered the feeling that we were peers, that he had faith in me as a professional. He gave me tough assignments and said, 'You can do this.' I felt I'd been given a precious trust.

"Ron gave the staff plenty of opportunities for hands-on experience with different phases of the work. The staff's testing began when Ron's brother Paul was diagnosed with cancer. Ron was flying back and forth between California and Denver to be with Paul, so the rest of us were filling in a lot. There was a real sadness about Ron at that time. He had always been such a fun-filled guy, and it was hard to see him go through this anxiety and grief.

"It was only about six months after Paul died that Ron came to the staff and announced he would be leaving to take a pastorate in the Bay area. That was scary. We knew there would be a big vacuum when he left. But it wasn't as big a vacuum as it might have been, because he had prepared us to handle it by giving us a lot of freedom within the boundaries of our responsibilities.

"In the last two churches where I've served, I've usually had at least one or two younger men working alongside me—interns, youth workers, or seminary students. I try to create the kind of peer relationship I had with Ron, so that they each have a lot of freedom yet accountability within the parameters of their jobs."

When we invest our trust in others, we affirm our confidence and faith in them. And that, in turn, gives them the self-confidence to try, to risk, and to grow.

DON'T DIMINISH THE COST

My best sport in high school and college was track. Unfortunately, the small college I attended for two years in the Midwest didn't have an experienced track coach. Instead, the basketball coach, who had little interest in track, was given the job of coaching the track team.

The first day he met with the track team, he told us, "Come out when you can and practice on your own. If you can't make it to practice, try to do some running in the evening or before school. I'm afraid I won't be out here very much, so I've typed up a sheet of suggested workouts for you."

Many of those who came out for the team quit after the first meeting. They were disillusioned, and even a little disgusted. No one wanted to be on a team without standards, without demands.

Happily, one of my teammates had an idea. "Why do we have to be on the school track team?" he said. "We could compete in the big meets just by forming a track *club*. We could coach each other. I bet we could motivate each other to be the best in the state!"

So we formed a track club and called ourselves the Council Bluffs Striders. We trained hard under a demanding self-imposed discipline. Unable to afford the colorful uniforms of the other schools, we spray-painted "Council Bluffs Striders" on our T-shirts. We worked and sweated our way to the Midwest AAU Finals, a huge meet with teams from all the midwestern states, and our team finished second in the two-mile relay.

In my high school days, I had a very demanding track coach, a mentor who knew well how to motivate his athletes. Our track team met twice a day. During the cold winter months, we ran until the capillaries in our throats broke and we spit blood. The coach had us run ten 440s in a row, each in under sixty seconds. He let us walk 100 yards, then started us all over again. It was hard, excruciating work, but no one complained. Every member of the team was motivated to endure the pain and win the prize.

Since my experiences on the track, I've always remembered that when you reduce the demand of involvement, you reduce the appeal of involvement, which is a crucial principle for the mentoring process: If we diminish the cost of serving Christ, we diminish the appeal of serving Christ. If we, as mentors, want to motivate our learners to more committed and sacrificial service to the cause of Christ, we must never reduce the demands of the challenge.

MAKE THEM FEEL LIKE WINNERS

At the same time, we need to recognize that making hard demands as a mentor does not mean being harsh with people. It doesn't mean we are to motivate by criticism, ridicule, or anger. Nothing squelches motivation like blame and criticism. And nothing engenders intrinsic motivation like encouragement and affirmation. As Thomas J. Peters and Robert H. Waterman, Jr., observe in their book, *In Search of Excellence,*

> Most organizations, we find, take a negative view of their people. They verbally berate participants for poor performance. (Most actually talk tougher than they act, but the tough talk nonetheless intimidates people.) They call for risk taking but punish even tiny failures. They want innovation but kill the spirit of the champion. . . . They design systems that seem calculated to tear down their workers' self-image. They might not mean to be doing that, but they are.[4]

Peters and Waterman found that *most* organizations try to motivate their people with negative, punitive, critical measures by means of fear and intimidation. I have seen such methods used to motivate people not only in secular businesses, but in companies operated by Christian businessmen, in Christian organizations, in churches, and even in one-on-one mentoring relationships. Moreover, I have seen the tragic results when such methods are applied: discouragement, bitterness, emo-

tional confusion, and a sense of worthlessness in the employee
or learner.

When we berate and criticize, we make the learner feel like a
loser. And when people *feel* like losers, they *become* losers.
Our task as mentors is to motivate our learners by *making them
feel like winners*.

About twenty years ago, Larry Olson (who is now pastor of
the First Presbyterian Church in Waukon, Iowa) assisted me as
youth pastor of a large church in Minneapolis. Larry was eigh-
teen years old and learning the ropes. Part of the way I tried to
mentor him was by edging myself out of leadership as spiritual
director of a singing group called the Children of Hope, while
gradually edging Larry in.

Larry was known to his friends as "Brillo," because of his
wooly, curly haircut. He lived in the manse next to the church
and, naturally, it was called Brillo's Pad. Larry was available
to young people with needs or questions literally twenty-four
hours a day. I learned a lot from Larry about what it means to
be a "three A.M. Christian," a full-time, twenty-four-hour
friend to others.

Today, Larry admits, "I wasn't much of a risk-taker. I didn't
really want to stretch myself in new directions. I liked to play it
safe." I could see that in Larry, but I could also see that Larry
had a lot more potential than he realized.

I encouraged Larry to try new jobs and projects that would
stretch him. Here's what Larry told Jim Denney about our
mentoring relationship: "Ron was always saying, 'You can do
this, Larry.' He was always challenging me to expand my potential, to go after things I had already stuffed in my 'I Can't
Do It' file. He wouldn't let me spend my life on anything less
than the best.

"Once he put me in charge of a Youth Specialties seminar he
had set up. Initially, I was his assistant, following him around
like a puppy dog, learning from him and being assigned little

jobs. Then something came up and Ron had to hand the whole thing off to me. I was terrified, but it came off all right and I learned a lot from it.

"I've had a number of mentors in my life. One taught me how to give to others and to God. Another showed me how to have fun in life, that Christianity is not just a bunch of rules and regulations. Ron taught me to take risks, to believe in myself."

I've found that the most effective way to motivate others is by encouraging them, by making them feel like winners. One of the most important dimensions of being a biblical mentor is that of being an *encourager*.

THE SON OF ENCOURAGEMENT

Next to Jesus Christ, my favorite New Testament character is a man named Barnabas. Even his name is appealing: *Bar,* meaning "son," and *Nabas,* meaning "encouragement"— literally "son of encouragement." This name was probably given him after his conversion to Christ in order to describe the kind of man he became after the Spirit of God transformed his heart. Barnabas was a mentor and a man who knew how to motivate his learners by encouraging them.

Every time you meet Barnabas in the New Testament, you find encouragement taking place. You first find him in Acts 11, described as "a good man, full of the Holy Spirit and of faith."[5] He was mentoring a new Christian convert named Saul—a convert who will later become Paul, a great evangelist, writer, missionary, and mentor in his own right.

In Acts 15, Barnabas took another young man into a mentoring relationship—John Mark, who accompanied Barnabas on his missionary journey to Cyprus and beyond. John Mark had accompanied Barnabas and the apostle Paul on a previous missionary journey and had failed. He had gone with the two men as far as Pamphylia (in present-day southern Turkey), and he had turned back, discouraged by the harsh deprivation and persecution they had encountered.

Paul, who could often be as tough and demanding as a Marine drill instructor, refused to give John Mark a second chance. Acts 15:38 records, "Paul *insisted* that they should not take with them the one who had departed from them in Pamphylia" (emphasis added). Barnabas the encourager, however, saw potential in John Mark. He saw a young man who had failed once, but who had learned from his failure, and who now approached life with more resolve and commitment than ever before. So Paul and Barnabas went their separate ways, Paul choosing Silas as his new partner, and Barnabas choosing to mentor John Mark.

Largely as a result of the encouragement and mentoring of Barnabas, John Mark later emerged as a key figure in the missionary expansion of the early church and as the author of the second of the four Gospels. And Paul, it seems, later ate his words of rejection toward John Mark. Late in his ministry, Paul wrote to Timothy, "Get Mark and bring him with you, *for he is useful to me for ministry,*"[6] (emphasis added), a concise recognition of the skills and character qualities built into John Mark by his mentor and motivator, the son of encouragement, Barnabas.

REJOICING WITH THE LEARNER

Being an encourager is not always as easy as it sounds. To be an authentic encourager, a mentor is often called upon, as Paul said, to "rejoice with those who rejoice, and weep with those who weep."[7]

My father was a man of great compassion, a man who would always rejoice with those who rejoiced and weep with those who wept. His greatest strengths as a pastor were at the bedside, at the graveside, or in the home of someone who was grieving or hurting. I learned from him long after the sermons were preached and the administrative work of a church done, what people *really* remembered about a pastor were the acts of Christlike compassion he had done for others.

I often saw him weep openly when he heard that a friend was critically ill or that someone in his congregation had died. And I also saw him rejoice with a couple who had just had a baby or a businessman who had just received a promotion or a farmer who was having a fruitful season.

Unfortunately, many of us find it a lot easier to weep with those who weep than to rejoice with those who rejoice. When someone else is weeping, we are in a superior position to them. They are in crisis, we are not. They are unemployed, we are not. They are grieving, we are not.

But when someone else gets a big promotion, an award, or a recognition—in short, when they are rejoicing—it's easy for us to become resentful and jealous. A biblical mentor must be secure enough not to feel threatened by the learner's progress and success. One test of our spiritual maturity is the way we answer this question: Can I authentically rejoice when another Christian brother or sister is experiencing growth, vitality, success, and joy?

To be effective, biblical mentors, we must be generous, always ready to affirm, always pulling for the learner and cheering him on, always motivating and encouraging, always hoping that the learner will not only catch us, but *surpass* us. Our goal as mentors is not simply to make carbon copies of ourselves, but to spur others on to even greater things than we ourselves have achieved.

Our model as mentors was the Master Mentor, the Master Motivator, who said of his own learners, "He who believes in Me, the works that I do he will do also; and greater works than these he will do, because I go to My Father."[8] Think of it: Jesus encouraged you and me to do even *greater* works than he himself did! With these words, the Master Mentor carved out a model for us in our own mentoring relationships. When our learners are energized to do even greater works than we can do, then we have done our job well.

Chapter 10

PERSEVERANCE
The blessing of criticism

"OLD BEARSKIN"

Knute Rockne was a coach and a mentor, the man who built the "Fighting Irish" of Indiana's Notre Dame University into a major power in college football. He pioneered the "platoon system" of substituting offensive and defensive teams during the game, which revolutionized both college and professional football. Under his leadership, Notre Dame won 103 out of 122 games in thirteen seasons, and for five of those seasons was undefeated. A colorful character with a great sense of humor, he was loved and respected by the young men he coached.

One day, a football column with the heading "Old Bearskin" appeared in the school paper. It was the vilest, most insulting piece of sports journalism ever to appear in print on the Notre Dame campus. It berated the team, insulting Rockne himself, as well as many of the team's star players.

The column continued appearing week after week, filled not only with vicious opinions but with inside information. One week, the column berated a star player as lazy and documented how he had lagged through practice. Another column depicted one player as cocky and arrogant and contained exact quotes of bragging statements this young man had made in the locker room. Another column contained a list of the players who had broken training. Another column described the scrapbook full of clippings that one of the players kept and read daily.

Clearly, there was a spy inside the team who was feeding information to "Old Bearskin."

"Coach, we've got to find this guy and fix him!" said Tom, the latest victim of "Old Bearskin," stomping into Rockne's office and waving a copy of the offending column.

"You're telling me!" Rockne raged. "Did you see what this guy wrote about me last week? Why, I've been libeled! I was over there just this morning, demanding to know the identity of this 'Bearskin' rascal, and the editor of the paper refuses to tell me who it is!"

"Well, what are we going to do, coach?"

"The only thing we *can* do, I guess," said Rockne. "Get out on that gridiron and show everyone in the state that this 'Bearskin' character doesn't know what he's talking about!"

That season, the fall of 1930, the Fighting Irish won every game they played. Sadly, it turned out to be Rockne's last season as coach. On March 31, 1931, Rockne was killed when an airplane in which he was a passenger crashed into a field in Chase County, Kansas.

After Rockne's death, the editor of the school paper revealed the identity of "Old Bearskin": Knute Rockne himself. He had used the column to keep his star players from becoming too conceited and impressed by the publicity and adulation they received. Determined to make a liar out of "Old Bearskin," the Fighting Irish were spurred on to achieve one last undefeated season for their coach—their beloved mentor and anonymous tormentor—before his untimely death.

". . . THE HEART OF A CHILD, THE HIDE OF A RHINOCEROS"

Criticism can be a blessing. Criticism can help make us more mature in Christ. This is not an easy thing for me to say, because I've experienced a great deal of criticism over the years. I know the intense pain of being harshly, bitterly accused of things I know are untrue. I know how it feels to have my motives and my integrity questioned. I know how it feels to know people are saying damaging things about me and my ministry, and to be completely powerless to set the record straight.

Yet I also know that the criticism I have received, no matter how harsh or how hurtful, whether there was any truth to it or whether it was based entirely on lies or misunderstanding, has served to make me stronger. I can say in all honesty that I have been able to become more mature in Christ even as a result of unfair and unloving criticism.

I am learning that part of the task of a biblical mentor is to help the learner endure criticism, grow stronger from it, and keep moving forward.

My brother Paul was a mentor who understood and exemplified what it means to persevere. As a coach, he often persevered against criticism. As a man, he persevered against the pain and fear of cancer. After his death in 1985, I visited Paul's wife and children in their Denver home. I walked into the room that had been his office, and there on his desk was a framed quotation by Theodore Roosevelt:

> It is not the critic who counts; not the man who points out how the strong man stumbled, or whether the doer of deeds could have done better.
> The credit belongs to the man who is actually in the arena;
> Whose face is marred by dust and sweat and blood; who strives valiantly; who errs and comes short again and again;

Who knows the great enthusiasms, the great devotions, and
spends himself in a worthy cause;

Who, at best knows in the end the triumph of high achievement;

And who at the worst, if he fails, at least fails while daring
greatly.

It is far better to dare mighty things, to win glorious tri-
umphs, even though checkered by failure, than to rank with
those poor spirits who neither enjoy nor suffer much because
they live in the gray twilight of life, knowing neither victory
nor defeat.

Misunderstanding and criticism are inevitable features in the
life of anyone who would attempt anything worthwhile for
God. That's why J. Oswald Sanders wrote in *Spiritual Leadership,* that no leader is exempt from criticism, and his humility
will nowhere be seen more clearly than in the manner in which
he accepts it and reacts to it. That's why Lorne Sanny of the
Navigators said the greatest problem the Christian leader will
have to endure is the problem of being misunderstood. And
that's why Stuart Briscoe observed that the three qualifications
for a Christian leader are the mind of a scholar, the heart of a
child, and the hide of a rhinoceros.

A pastor, fresh out of seminary, was devastated by the vindictive criticism he received early in his first pastorate. Fortunately, this young pastor had a mentor, an older, more
experienced pastor named Fred Mitchell. At one particularly
discouraging point in his ministry, the younger man received
this letter from Pastor Mitchell:

My dear friend and colleague,

I am glad to know that you are taking any blessing that can be found in the criticism brought
against you by one of your parishioners, in which
case even his bitter attack will yield sweetness in
your ministry.

A sentence which has been of great help to Mrs. Mitchell and myself is this: *It does not matter what happens to us, but our reaction to what happens to us is of vital importance.*

I think you must expect more and more criticism, for with increasing responsibility, this is inevitable. It causes one to walk humbly with God and to take such action as God alone desires for you.

Yours in Christ,
Fred Mitchell

What a key truth for all of us who face the sting of criticism and misunderstanding: It doesn't matter what happens to us, but our reaction to what happens to us is vitally important.

And what an encourager this mentor was to his young learner! Each of us, in our mentoring relationships, should strive to be like this man: involved in our learner's struggles, encouraging him or her to persevere and respond to those struggles with grace and courage, strengthening the learner to face the trials ahead.

PERSEVERANCE IN THE BIBLE

People of vision, people who seek to build, people who seek to move forward, are the inevitable targets of critics. You see it in the lives of great achievers in the 1990s, and you see it in the lives of the great men and women of Scripture. The most compelling example of all was Christ himself, who endured not only opposition and criticism, but paid the ultimate price: death by crucifixion.

The apostle Paul endured opposition and criticism not only from enemies of the faith, but from people within the early Christian church itself. To Timothy, he wrote about the persecutions he endured at Antioch, at Iconium, at Lystra,[1] and of the opposition of Alexander the coppersmith and Hymenaeus, former church leaders. Alexander was so vindictive toward Paul that he journeyed all the way from Ephesus to Rome, just to testify against Paul at his trial.[2]

The apostle John mentioned a man named Diotrephes, whom he described as "prating against us with malicious words. And not content with that, he himself does not receive the brethren, and forbids those who wish to, putting them out of the church."[3] Diotrephes was a critical, unloving "church boss" who demanded that the church be run his way, and he defamed, insulted, and chased off those who disagreed with him.

The Old Testament prophet Nehemiah persevered against intense criticism as he was seeking to rebuild the walls of Jerusalem. His principle critics were two men: Sanballat the Horonite and Tobiah the Ammonite official. The opposition begins in Nehemiah chapter 2, as Sanballat and Tobiah laugh derisively at Nehemiah. Then, in chapter 4, comes more ridicule.

Sanballat: "What are these feeble Jews doing? . . . Will they revive the stones from the heaps of rubbish?"

Tobiah: "Whatever they build, if even a fox goes up on it, he will break down their stone wall."[4]

In chapter 7, the opposition gets more serious and more dangerous. Sanballat and Tobiah see that Nehemiah is achieving his goals, so they plot with others to ambush and kill Nehemiah. When this plot fails, they spread lies that Nehemiah and his people are plotting to rebel against King Artaxerxes, and that Nehemiah wants to set himself up as king of the Jews—all lies and slander!

Nehemiah's response to the criticism, the lies, and the conspiracy against him are a model of how we as mentors and learners should respond when criticism comes our way: he went to his knees in prayer, and he continued to move ahead.

On a trip to Africa, I saw something which symbolized to me a persevering, Nehemiah-like response to opposition. Our Jeep was bouncing along through a game preserve in Kenya when we came upon a herd of wildebeest. The wildebeest (also known as a gnu) is a big, brawny relative of the antelope which lives in the grasslands of central and southern Africa. Our driver stopped the Jeep and we watched as two bull wildebeest squared off against each other for battle. Now, whether this battle was a form of wildebeest play or a serious struggle for leadership of the herd, I don't know. But what I saw was this: both of these fearsome, massive, horned animals faced each other, snorting and tossing their heads, hooves pawing the ground. Then something unexpected happened—both wildebeests *dropped to their knees* for a moment. Then they were up again, springing forward, charging ahead, persevering against opposition.

We would do well to emulate the wildebeest whenever we are attacked—drop to our knees in prayer, then spring forward and keep moving ahead. That's perseverance.

COURAGE UNDER FIRE

To persevere means, essentially, "to hold up courageously under fire." The longer I live out my life, the more convinced I become that perseverance is the central ingredient of all successful endeavors and the most important ingredient a mentor can pass on to a learner. It is an ingredient in all too short a supply in the human race.

The average person folds up and runs away when things get difficult. You and I must learn to persevere and to teach perseverance to those we seek to influence. The average person quits after two or three attempts. You and I must learn to try and try and try again until we reach the goal. And we must teach this same quality to those we seek to influence. The average person shrinks from criticism. You and I must learn to endure it, grow through it, and teach our learners how to do the same.

There will always be critics. As long as we are trying to build, there will be someone else trying to tear down. Habitual critics resist change, even if that change is for the good and for the betterment of the kingdom of God. Most habitual critics are insecure. They feel threatened by the success of others, and sometimes simply threatened by things that are new or unfamiliar.

Critics don't like to be around encouragers, because encouragers refuse to feed on the verbal pollution they like to spew. So critics tend to gravitate toward other critics. In the case of Nehemiah's critics, what was Sanballat without Tobiah? What was Tobiah without Sanballat? In your own life, you will likely find that your own critics won't oppose you singly so much as in pairs or in packs.

Nehemiah was a mentor, an encourager, a motivator. He ultimately succeeded in getting the wall built. His opponents, Tobiah and Sanballat, were critics. The difference between these two kinds of people is the difference between midnight and noonday. Mentors encourage, inspire, and achieve great goals. Critics demoralize and destroy.

Having said all this, we must make a careful distinction between habitual critics and those who care enough to courageously, constructively, lovingly criticize our behavior for our own good. The mark of both a biblical mentor and a sincere learner is a willingness to listen when a godly person comes reflecting the tender-tough love of Jesus Christ. When another person takes the risk—and it is a risk!—of illuminating one of our blind spots, then we owe it to that person to receive that criticism, reflect on it, and pray about it. The criticism may or may not be valid, but the love behind that kind of gentle, compassionate criticism is *always* valid. If we sense even a kernel of truth in that criticism, we will act on it, because our goal is to continue to become more like the Master Mentor, Jesus Christ.

But there was nothing godly about Nehemiah's critics, Tobiah and Sanballat. You may be facing such ungodly attacks right now.

Tragically, some of the harshest and most ungodly criticism we will ever face may come from other Christians. I have seen two believers who agree on 95 percent of everything regarding Christian faith, doctrine, and practice become absolutely vindictive and irreconcilable toward each other over that tiny 5 percent of disagreement. As Charles Caleb Colton once observed, "In religion and politics, we seem to have less love for those who believe half our creed than for those who deny the whole of it."

Some sobering statistics regarding the way we treat each other as Christians: Out of any given seminary graduating class, 20 percent will quit the ministry and find some other career within five years of entering the ministry. And what do you think is the number one reason these pastors leave the ministry? Not low pay. Not moral problems. Not health reasons. No, the number one reason pastors leave the ministry is the pressure of *criticism*.

STRENGTH UNDER CONTROL

How, then, should we respond when we are confronted by harsh, unloving criticism? One biblical truth which I have found a faithful guide in times of criticism is Proverbs 15:1: "A soft answer turns away wrath, but a harsh word stirs up anger." This doesn't mean that we should be doormats, or that we should allow ourselves to be manipulated by our critics. As mentors, we should exemplify strength, and we should seek to instill strength in the learner—but always *strength under control*.

When we react to criticism defensively (or, as many of us are prone to do, offensively), we set in motion an escalating cycle of anger and accusation. But we can break that cycle before it starts by heeding the biblical admonition, "A soft answer turns away wrath." As biblical mentors, we choose to reply to ungodly criticism softly, with honesty, with tender toughness, with Christlike controlled strength.

We reject retaliation. We reject resentment. We go to our knees in prayer, then we get up and move ahead. We persevere—both through the circumstances and *in love and forgiveness*.

In his book *Love, Acceptance & Forgiveness,* Jerry Cook soberly forewarned us,

> Jesus was crucified at the end of His ministry, and it was the equivalent of the local ministerial association that put Him on the cross. The religious community may put you on the cross too. If so, pray that God will forgive them, for they know not what they do. The very brothers who would crucify you may also fall some day, and when they do, they should be able to come to you and find love, acceptance and forgiveness.[5]

From my own experience, I can say that these are words to live by. As long as we are seeking to achieve things for Christ, you and I will be subject to criticism. And some of the toughest critics we will ever have to face may be our own brothers and sisters in Christ. It is in those times when it is the hardest to love and forgive that our ability to give Christlike unconditional love is truly tested.

THE PRICE OF MENTORING: CRITICISM

During the time this book was being written, I received an angry, critical letter from a parishioner. Many of the words in that letter were hurtful, but the lines that stung the most were these:

> You seem so warm and caring in the pulpit on Sunday mornings. Yet during the week you are almost

> completely unavailable. When I phone your office,
> I have to go through a receptionist and an adminis-
> trative assistant just to be told you'll return my call
> the next day. I'm left wondering which is the *real*
> Ron Davis—the sympathetic, compassionate man
> in the pulpit, or the one who's too busy to take my
> phone call.

I try to be certain the person I am in the pulpit is the same person I am at the office, on the street, and in the home. Still I have lived for years with the criticism that I am inaccessible. While I am continually trying to find ways to make myself more available to my congregation, I have to face that if I (a) pastor a congregation of 2,300 people, (b) devote two week-days to study and sermon preparation, and most of the rest of the week to staff meetings and scheduled appointments, and (c) commit large blocks of time to mentoring relationships, some people will be dissatisfied with the level of my accessibil-ity. It is *inevitable*. And even though this is by far the most common criticism I receive, I never get used to receiving a letter like the one I just quoted. Such criticism always stings.

The mentoring philosophy, which calls us to invest our lives in a few people, always yields great rewards. But there is a cost: The mentoring life-style almost always yields great criti-cism. There will be people who will not understand why you spend so much time with just a few individuals.

I'm thankful to say I do not receive nearly as much criticism for my mentoring life-style as I did in past years. There were times during previous pastorates when I experienced intense criticism, much of which was centered on my approach to mentoring.

On one occasion, two church leaders came to me on their own initiative and said, "Ron, in order to be successful in this church, you have to spend more time with the people. You need to spend more time in different committee meetings, at different church functions, and in the church office. That means you'll have to cut back the amount of time you spend in one-to-one times and retreats with the church staff. That also means you won't have as much time to spend with your family. That may sound hard, but that's just a sacrifice you make when you become a pastor."

When I refused to sacrifice my family, my staff relationships, and my mentoring relationships on the altar of committee meetings, public functions, and the expectations of my critics, the opposition toward my ministry increased. Certainly, that opposition centered around *several* issues, but a *key* issue was my personal commitment to relationships versus a consuming, workaholic "involvement."

During difficult days in my ministry, I have always been grateful to have a few intensely bonded friendships on the church staff. One of those friends is Mike Flavin. Mike told Jim Denney, "It is hard anytime Ron sees me and others on the staff experience criticism. He is like a father hurting for his children. And that's a sobering lesson to me as I try to be a mentor to others. A true mentor risks getting hurt. In addition to his own pain, a mentor sometimes has to endure a lot of vicarious pain through the people he mentors."

Joe Pettit, another colleague, remembers our ministry together: "My mentoring relationship with Ron was concentrated into a $2^{1}/_{2}$-year period. I say 'concentrated,' because that period was largely characterized by an atmosphere of crisis management, which tends to compress and accelerate the growth process.

"As soon as I came aboard, I felt a spontaneous affinity with Ron. It wasn't long before I felt I knew him well. There was a natural openness in him that made me feel I was instantly a part of his life, his work, his space. Even though we've since moved on to different places, he continues to nurture our friendship.

"If I have one critique of Ron as a mentor, it would be that he carries burdens on his own shoulders that he could share with others. It's not that he's closed or emotionally isolated—quite the contrary, he's very much an open book. But he's not a complainer. During times of conflict, he suffered a lot of things silently and alone that I tried to encourage him to lay open, to resolve in a more public way.

"He could get into the pulpit and confront sin and evil like a tiger. Yet, when he was sinned against, he tended to absorb it rather than confront it. As Ron himself admits, his 'tenderness' needed to be more strongly balanced by 'toughness.'"

To be effective, a mentor must be willing to persevere under pressure and criticism. Many people will question your commitment to invest yourself in a few. If you practice the strategy of the Master, you must expect to be misunderstood and criticized.

THE BATTLE IS THE LORD'S

I suspect everyone's favorite Bible story about opposition has to be the story of David and Goliath, probably because we all tend to identify with the little shepherd boy David and we all tend to see our opposition as Goliath-sized giants. When David went out to face Goliath, armed only with a sling and a few smooth stones, he said something to his opponent that often comes back to me whenever I face opposition: "The battle is the LORD's."[6]

As he prepares to face the giant, David is at peace, knowing that the battle belongs not to him, but to God. Whenever I am faced with opposition and evil criticism, I always remember, "The battle is the Lord's."

In 1983, I returned from my first trip to Africa having witnessed heartbreaking poverty and famine, having held dying, malnourished babies in my arms, having learned that 40,000 children were starving to death every day. My heart was heavy, and I wanted to communicate the urgency of the crisis to other Christians here in America.

As co-chairman of a community-wide "Love Africa" project to raise funds to help alleviate the suffering, I met with members of the media, with community leaders, and with many Christians groups, churches, and individuals. I shared with them the tragedy I had seen with my own eyes and showed them pictures that my traveling companions had taken. Then came the shock of the questioning:

"So what if we donate food or money, Ron? It won't really get there, will it?"

"Why feed a child today, Ron? Won't that same child just starve tomorrow?"

"Why spend all this money on food, Ron? Isn't it much more important to feed their souls than to feed their bellies?"

These are the questions that barraged me and my colleagues as we attempted to make a difference for those suffering the African famine. I was surprised to learn how many people, including Christians, criticized this effort. I finally reached a point where I had to simply kneel down before the Lord and say, "Jesus, I am willing to tell the story. I'm willing to describe what we saw when we flew into those villages in those bush planes. I'm willing to describe the heroic efforts of the Christian missionaries who were willing to pay the price to bring the compassion of Jesus into the heart of Africa and to make a difference for eternity. But, Lord, the battle is yours, not mine. I can't fight this battle. All I can do is persevere and leave the results to you."

Nehemiah persevered in his project of rebuilding the walls of Jerusalem. He could have said, "Gee, I didn't realize it was going to be so hard! I didn't know there would be all this opposition and ridicule! If I'd known it was going to be like this, I'd have just stayed in that plush palace in Susa! Who needs the hassle? I'm throwing in the towel!"

Not Nehemiah. He persevered. He got the job done.

Nehemiah could have said, along with the apostle Paul, "We are hard pressed on every side, yet not crushed; we are perplexed, but not in despair; persecuted, but not forsaken; struck down, but not destroyed."[7]

WHAT DOES IT TAKE TO STOP YOU?

Let me ask you a hard question: What does it take to stop you? An unkind word? A little unfair treatment? A little smudge on your reputation? A voice raised in anger? A threat against your job? A threat against your life? Where on that continuum of opposition do you run out of persistence and courage? At what point do you throw in the towel and give up? At what point do you just say, "Jesus, I give up. This is just too hard for me."

What does it take to stop you?

The difference between success and failure, between achievement and collapse, between having an impact on others for Christ and having no influence at all comes down to just one word: *perseverance.*

Several years ago, during a time of intense criticism and opposition in my ministry, my friend Jeff Baggett sent me a note of encouragement. A C. S. Lewis buff, Jeff thought I might be encouraged to know a little bit of what Lewis went through in his life. He was right; I was. Here is what Jeff wrote to me:

> C. S. Lewis' life has always had a greater impact on me than his writings.
>
> For nearly thirty years he was blackballed by the Oxford administrators and fellow staff from obtaining full professorship because of some misunderstanding. He was merely a tutor all those

years he was at Oxford. Yet he continued in the task for which he felt called by God.

Fueled by his intellectual gifts, he persevered and continued to write. C. S. Lewis' greatest works emerged out of those years of greatest opposition. He was openly criticized and despised by his peers for spending all of his energy on Christian writing. Yet in the outside world, his views and ideas were the most popular of the day, or of any day.

The Screwtape Letters appeared in 1942, at the apex of the criticism and opposition against him. On top of all of this were his personal losses: his mother's death, his rejection by his father, the death of his best army companion, the sudden death of his life-long friend Charles Williams in 1945, and the agonizing death, the result of cancer, of his wife Joy Davidman Lewis.

C. S. Lewis, in the midst of criticism and opposition and tragedy, continued to persevere for Jesus Christ.

You and I may not possess the brilliant intellect of C. S. Lewis. We may not be able to capture the hearts and imaginations of generations as he did. We may not be able to communicate biblical truth as eloquently and persuasively as he did. But we can persevere as he did. We can hold up courageously under fire.

Our goal as mentors is to learn to endure criticism, to keep moving forward, and to model perseverance before those who are watching our example.

PART THREE:

DEEPER DIMENSIONS OF MENTORING

Chapter 11

SOMETIMES IT HURTS

Facing problems and tensions in the mentoring relationship

THE BETRAYAL

Ben and his mentor Jonathan sat in a restaurant booth, sipping coffee, pouring syrup over their pancakes, enjoying each other's company, sharing together. While he was not Ben's immediate superior, Jonathan was an officer at the insurance company where Ben worked, as well as an elder in the church where Ben grew up. Jonathan had taken a big brother-type interest in Ben, and had even helped set up the job interview when the younger man was hired two years earlier.

"So, Ben," said Jonathan, "what can I be praying with you about this week?"

"If I could share something in strict confidence—"

"Sure, sure, Ben! What is it?"

"It's about my work with the company," Ben started, then bit his lip, hesitating. "I'm up for a promotion, and Sally and I really need that raise with the baby coming. It would really hurt my chances if it got around that I've got this problem—"

"Hey, don't give it another thought," the older man assured warmly. "I just want to support you and be praying for you."

"I appreciate that," said Ben. "The problem is I've had a lot of trouble getting myself organized. I feel really scattered lately. I'm working nights, weekends, coming in early, taking work home, trying to catch up. I think I'll make it with the extra effort I'm putting in. But I'd really appreciate it if you'd pray for me and hold me accountable in the area of sharpening my organizational skills."

"That's what I'm here for, Ben."

They prayed together, then Jonathan picked up the check.

Later in the week, Ben was at his desk when Pete, his immediate superior at the company, stopped by. Pete's face looked drawn and serious. "Hi, Ben," he said somberly.

"Hi, Pete," Ben said, leaning back in his chair. "Say, you don't look so good."

"Well," said Ben's boss, "this is my 'bad news' face."

Ben's own expression fell. "Oh, no. Don't tell me. I didn't get the promotion."

Pete sighed. "That's right. No promotion. The personnel meeting was this morning. I was in there pitching for you, but . . ." He trailed off, shrugging. "It's a shame. Your work's really been improving lately. I tried to tell the big guys you've been giving the company 110 percent, but they still gave the promotion thumbs down." He hesitated, then said, "By the way, I thought Jonathan was a friend of yours."

"What do you mean?" said Ben. "Of course he's my friend. He practically got me this job."

Pete gave Ben a pitying look. "Yeah? Well, he's the one who nixed your promotion."

"He *what?*" Ben sat bolt upright in his chair.

"In the personnel meeting this morning. I was right there. Jonathan told everybody in the room how disorganized you are. He said you told him yourself how scattered you've been. Your 'good friend' torpedoed you, Ben."

Ben had trusted his mentor, and his mentor had betrayed him. Yet trust goes both ways in a mentoring relationship.

Sometimes it is the mentor who is betrayed by the learner, as a pastor named Rev. Stone found out.

A MENTOR BETRAYED

Nineteen-year-old Cindy Turner sat on the sofa in Rev. Stone's counseling room. The pastor set two glasses of iced tea on the coffee table and seated himself across from Cindy.

"Cindy," said Pastor Stone, "would you lead us in prayer?"

She nodded and closed her eyes. "Dear Father," she said, "I thank you for the many wonderful weeks I've had as a youth ministry intern in this church, for all the special people in this church who have been so supportive of me, for the junior high and high school kids I've learned to know and love, and especially for the mentoring relationship you've built between myself and Pastor Stone, this man who has invested in me and taught me so much about what it means to be a servant to you and to others. Bless this hour that we spend together. In Jesus' name—" and they both said, "Amen."

For most of the remaining hour, Cindy and Pastor Stone talked together, evaluating Cindy's work (which was consistently excellent), her attitude (which was unfailingly positive), and her rapport with the young people and their parents (which was superb). Toward the end of their time together, Pastor Stone said, "Since you'll be leaving us in just two weeks, I wanted you to know how much you'll be missed by this church. I don't know when we've had a youth ministry intern who was so deeply and unanimously loved by the congregation."

Cindy smiled shyly. "Well . . . thank you."

"I mean every word," Pastor Stone continued. "I really see that the Lord has great things planned for your future. The youth ministry has more than doubled since you came here. You've brought so many creative ideas into the program—the Concert in the Park, the Christmas Carnival, the Snow Blast. And not only are you creative, but you have the administrative and leadership skills to carry out those ideas successfully.

When you've finished your education, I hope you'll give me a call, because there'll be a full-time staff position waiting for you whenever you're ready."

The following week, Pastor Stone was in his office when he received a call from Steve Howard, in whose home Cindy stayed during her internship. "Pastor," he said, "I sure hate to tell you this. Last night, my wife found Cindy passed out in her room."

"Passed out?" said Pastor Stone. "You mean she was sick?"

"I mean she was . . . drunk."

Pastor Stone nearly fumbled the phone.

"The room reeked of alcohol," Mr. Howard went on. "We found several empty liquor bottles under the bed."

Pastor Stone's stomach clenched like a big fist. He swallowed hard. "Could there be any mistake about this?"

Just then, Cindy went past the open door of his study. She smiled and waved, then disappeared down the hall.

On the phone, Mr. Howard's voice quavered. "There's no mistake. The worst of it is that my daughter Lisa has known about it for weeks. Lisa found her drunk one time, and Cindy swore her to secrecy."

In the weeks that followed, Pastor Stone spent hours dealing with the issue of Cindy's alcohol problem: counseling with the Howards and their daughter; meeting with the church board and pastoral staff as they sorrowfully decided how Cindy should be disciplined; meeting with angry or disillusioned parishioners. At a special congregational meeting, the board announced Cindy's resignation for reasons involving "serious errors in judgment," yet word of Cindy's alcohol problem leaked out and became a scandal in the church.

Pastor Stone never imagined he could feel so let down and disillusioned. Cindy was so gifted and had such a great future ahead of her. How could this have happened?

A mentoring relationship lives on trust. When that trust is

betrayed, the relationship dies. What do you do as a mentor when a learner lets you down and betrays the trust you have placed in him or her? Do you wash your hands of that person? Turn your back?

Pastor Stone didn't. Despite all the pain, trouble, and disappointment Cindy had caused him, Pastor Stone met with her, prayed with her, and counseled her during the last few days before she returned home. He also made a number of phone calls to help arrange counseling and medical care for her chemical dependency.

Pastor Stone didn't dispense cheap grace. Rather, he encouraged Cindy to realistically shoulder the responsibility for her own actions. And Cindy, to her credit, confessed her own responsibility in tears of genuine sorrow. Pastor Stone helped Cindy work through the guilt over the hurt she had caused herself and so many others so that she could begin the tough climb back toward wholeness and a sense of forgiveness. Most important of all, Pastor Stone helped Cindy to see that, even though she would have to live with the consequences of her sin, she still had a useful life ahead of her.

Even when the mentoring relationship is ended, Christian love goes on.

FINE-TUNING THE RELATIONSHIP

Like husband-wife, parent-child, and other human relationships, the mentor-learner relationship has its ups and downs, its joys and its strains. Mentoring relationships require work, thought, care, and nurture.

Tim was a newly-hired writer for a national religious magazine. In his early twenties, fresh out of college, with just three years of college newspaper experience under his belt, Tim was placed under the tutelage of an experienced Christian editor named Mr. Finch. Tim considered his mentoring relationship with Mr. Finch a rare privilege. He had read several of the

books his mentor had written, and considered the opportunity
to work side-by-side with him the chance of a lifetime.

Every day, Tim learned something new about the writing and
editing business as Mr. Finch gave him assignments, critiqued
and edited his writing, and told him stories from his many
years in the publishing business. Tim found his mentor's criticism of his work to be frank but fair, and he appreciated that.
Over the weeks, Tim and Mr. Finch developed a warm and
mutually respectful friendship.

One day, just three months after he had been hired, Mr.
Finch appeared at the door of Tim's office. "Just read your
article, Tim," the older man said.

"What did you think?"

Mr. Finch tossed the manuscript onto Tim's desk. "I think
it's lousy. You completely missed the main point I wanted you
to cover. The lead is boring. And it's all choppy, no flow to it at
all. I'm really disappointed, Tim. Do it over." With that, Mr.
Finch turned his back and started to walk away.

"Hey!"

Mr. Finch turned around, his brow raised in surprise. Tim
had risen to his feet, snatched up the manuscript, and was
shaking it at Mr. Finch. "'It's lousy'?!" Tim snarled. "What
kind of constructive criticism is that? 'It's lousy'! I wrote it the
way you told me to write it! That lead paragraph is great the
way it is, and the whole piece flows just fine! In fact, it's one of
the best pieces I've ever done! So if you want someone to do it
over, get someone else to do it!" With that, Tim angrily flung
the manuscript toward Mr. Finch. It fluttered to the floor at the
editor's feet like a wounded dove.

In a low but threatening tone Mr. Finch replied, "If I say it's
lousy, then it's lousy. If I say do it over, then you had better do it
over. And if you want to get along around here, mister, you had
better exhibit more professional conduct." He turned and

walked away, leaving the manuscript huddled on the floor.

Tim slumped in his chair. He was furious with Mr. Finch. But he was even more furious with himself. A few minutes later, he stood hesitantly before the closed door of Mr. Finch's office. He knocked.

"Come in."

Tim entered. "Mr. Finch, I wanted to say—"

"Oh, it's you," the editor said gruffly. "Why aren't you at your word processor?"

"I came to apologize."

"Just rewrite that piece," said Mr. Finch. "If you're too cocky to take editorial criticism from someone with thirty years' experience in this business, then—"

"You're absolutely right, Mr. Finch," Tim said hastily. "You have every right to be angry with me. I can't believe I blew up like that. I mean, it was like part of me was standing in amazement, watching this crazy person yell at one of the most admired and respected men I know. It's just that when you said, 'It's lousy,' I felt exactly like I did when I was a little kid and my dad would tell me how stupid I was. When you turned around and started to walk away, it was just like when my dad used to turn his back on me. It always made me feel so worthless and ashamed." Tim fell silent for a moment, realizing he had said more than he meant to say. "Anyway," he finished, "I just want you to know it won't happen again. I was wrong, and I'm really sorry."

Mr. Finch sat silently, frowning, for what seemed like an eternity. "I shouldn't have criticized your article so harshly," he said at last. "I don't know why I did that. . . . Actually, I guess I do know. I had a big fight with my son this morning. Maybe I just had it in for any guy that reminded me of my own boy. Why don't you bring that article back in here? I'll read it again. I think I can be more objective now. And I'll criticize it *constructively* this time."

Tim grinned and turned to leave.

"Oh, and Tim—" Mr. Finch added, his eyes moist. "Thanks for coming in."

Anger and conflict are often part of a mentoring relationship. That's why forgiveness and empathy must also be a part of the mentoring process.

Both the mentor and the learner must be alert to hidden symbols in the mentoring relationship. It's easy for a learner to unconsciously see the mentor as a symbolic parent, and for the mentor to see the learner as a symbolic child. In many ways, a mentor assumes a role much deeper than that of a mere teacher or trainer, a role with strong parental resonances. In a very real sense, he or she becomes a guide/caretaker/nurturer of the learner's soul.

If the learner has powerful and unresolved areas of hurt or conflict with his or her parents, or if the mentor is unconsciously wrestling with inner ghosts or broken memories, there will likely be some pain and conflict in the mentoring relationship. Mentors and learners bring more than their hopes, attitudes, beliefs, and skills to the relationship. They also bring their brokenness and unresolved issues.

So both the learner and the mentor must be alert to the possibility of hidden issues on both sides of the relationship. Both partners in the process must look within and ask, "Am I responding to this person as he or she really is? Or am I reacting to a hidden symbol—a parent or a child—from my past?" And each partner in the process must seek to understand the other: "Could it be that this mentor or this learner is not really reacting in anger toward me but toward some person I represent to his or her unconscious mind?"

A mentoring relationship feeds on trust, breathes in an atmosphere of honesty and openness, and is nurtured and maintained with forgiveness and unconditional love. When a problem arises in the relationship, both the learner and mentor should treat that problem as part of the learning and growing experience of the mentoring process. We all have our rough edges, and a certain amount of conflict and creative tension in the mentoring relationship can be just the abrasive we need to sand those rough edges down and make us more like Christ.

But sometimes a mentoring relationship exhibits deeper problems, requiring more radical treatment.

MALIGNANT PERSONALITIES

Eric was a summer intern in a large church in the Midwest. In this internship program, each of the three or four college students in the program was assigned a mentor. Eric's mentor was an elder named Mr. Williamson.

Eric was put to work with primary-age Sunday school, Vacation Bible School, and several other areas of the church ministry. He lived in the Williamson home, where he was expected to carry out a heavy load of chores, including babysitting and bathing the children when the Williamsons were out, mowing the half-acre Williamson lawn, and even waiting table when the Williamsons entertained important guests. A typical day for Eric began at 6:00 A.M. and continued nonstop until he fell exhausted into his bed at 1:00 or 2:00 A.M. that night.

"Mr. Williamson," Eric said at the end of the third week, "I don't see how I can keep up this pace. I haven't had more than four hours of sleep a night since I've been here. It's really killing me."

"Look, Eric," Mr. Williamson replied, "if you want me to pray with you that God would give you more endurance, fine. But you came here to learn, and it looks like the first thing you have to learn is that you have to be willing to pay the price. When you're really sold out to God, then you don't whine about how tired you are."

Eric decided not to bring up the subject anymore. And though Eric continually tried to avoid conflict with his mentor,

Mr. Williamson determinedly turned every discussion into a contest between Eric's opinions and his. If Eric stood his ground on any issue, Mr. Williamson reminded Eric that he had sacrificially invested his time and opened his home to Eric, and that he was older and more experienced than Eric. This young man found himself feeling guilty simply for having his own ideas and convictions.

The one bright spot in Eric's summer was a buoyant and charming young lady with red hair and blue eyes. Like Eric, Lana was a summer intern. Eric was ecstatic when Lana agreed to go out with him for a movie and Cokes. But when he asked Mr. Williamson for an evening off, the older man replied, "You can't go out with Lana."

Eric was dismayed. "Why? Is there a church policy about interns dating each other?"

"No," said Mr. Williamson. "I simply don't think you and Lana would be right for each other."

"You mean *you* are telling me who I can and cannot date? *You* are making that decision for my life?"

"It's my responsibility to look after your welfare, to guide you, so that you don't make a major mistake with your life. It's a responsibility I take very seriously, Eric."

Eric was angry and hurt, but remembering a pledge he had signed when he first arrived at the beginning of the summer, he decided to submit to his mentor's authority for the duration of his internship.

Bound by a commitment he had made without knowing what he was in for, Eric showed great strength of character in submitting to the situation for the rest of the summer. But he paid a price. At the end of that summer, he was disillusioned about a career in the ministry, so much so that he changed his major upon returning to college and has since become a public school teacher.

Almost ten years after that difficult summer, Eric now looks back on it as a painful but positive influence on his life. "What happened to me was wrong, but the Lord can use even unjust experiences to make a person stronger. The sad thing is that those experiences also make a person more hardened and cynical. I've had other mentors since Mr. Williamson, but I've become more wary in those kinds of relationships. The happy ending is that Lana and I have been very happily married for the past eight years."

Eric's advice to anyone in a relationship with a mentor like Mr. Williamson: "Get out. Fast."

If there is a tendency on the part of the mentor to try to control, manipulate, and clone the learner, as in the relationship between Eric and Mr. Williamson, or if there is a lack of confidentiality and trust, as in the relationship between Ben and his mentor Jonathan, then the mentoring relationship is useless. To continue the relationship may actually result in spiritual and emotional harm to the learner.

That doesn't mean that the learner should not forgive the malignant mentor or that the learner has nothing to learn from the experience. In fact, it may well be that the most important lesson God has for us when we find ourselves in a mentoring relationship with a malignant personality is the lesson that we *must* forgive, we *must* learn the lessons of the experience, and we *must* pick ourselves up and get on with our lives in order to grow toward greater spiritual and emotional wholeness.

MANY MENTORS

If there is one peril I see in the mentoring process, it is the danger that mentors will seek to make disciples of themselves rather than of Christ and that learners will seek to become replicas of their mentors rather than imitators of Christ. We should view it as a warning sign, a danger sign, if we detect in ourselves a tendency to idolize a single mentor.

This is no hypothetical danger I am posing. I have seen more than one mentoring relationship succumb to it. What is most frightening of all is that it is so easy for us to *think* we are imitating Christ when, in fact, we are merely copying some weak, fallible, human idol.

A friend on the East Coast recently told me about a man named Jack, a stockbroker in New England. Now in his early thirties, Jack has been in a mentoring relationship for many years with a very successful financier named Wayne. Once, about ten years ago, Jack had said, "I want to be just like Wayne—have the kind of values he has, have a house like his, dress like him, everything."

Certainly, Jack had plenty of reason to admire many of Wayne's qualities. Wayne was a strong and active leader in the church they both attended, as well as a leader in the community. Wayne had even served a term as an alderman in their township.

Unfortunately, Wayne used his wealth to get his way in the church. He had an intimidating personality, and a number of people had left the church after a run-in with him.

Equally unfortunate was the fact that Jack assimilated many of his mentor's flaws as well as his strengths. Today, Jack is wealthy and successful like his hero, Wayne. Also like Wayne, Jack has become a power-broker and an intimidating figure in the church.

Herein lies the danger of idolizing our mentors. We should seek to view our mentors respectfully, but also objectively. Our goal is to discover and assimilate the Christlike qualities of our mentors and to discard anything that doesn't resemble the Master Mentor. Our goal is to become all we are meant to be in Christ, not to become clones.

One way to make sure that we avoid the excesses and extremes of a single mentor with an aberrant or malignant personality is to make sure that we have *many* mentors, not just one. I always encourage those who are learning alongside me to seek to learn from a wide range of experiences and a wide variety of mentors. I try to expose those who are learning alongside me to varied approaches, ideas, and personalities.

Not only do I urge others to have many mentors, but I try to live out my own advice. In addition to the many mentors whose examples I continue to emulate and whose counsel I continue to seek, I meet with a group of five men in my own church every Wednesday morning for breakfast, prayer, and sharing. I seek the perspective of these men on all the crucial decisions and tough judgment calls in my personal and professional life.

In these five men, I have found all the mentoring attributes I have outlined in this book—integrity, wisdom, motivation, perseverance, and most of all, tender toughness. I want to be surrounded by strong, caring mentors, not "yes-men." I want to be surrounded by men who will support me in the hard times, but who won't hesitate to disagree with me and even confront me if they see me straying from God's will.

These men come from varying backgrounds, age levels, and professions. They offer a diverse range of viewpoints and experience. They hold me accountable and keep me on course. They are a mirror, reflecting my inner self so that I can understand myself better.

Every biblical mentor has something to teach us about what it means to be a follower of Jesus Christ. Every biblical mentor has a piece of the puzzle. But no human being on earth has the entire puzzle. No mentor exemplifies the full spectrum of Christlike character. To become all we were meant to be in Christ, we need not one, but *many* mentors.

THE BLESSING

Alex was a young associate pastor in his midtwenties, working in a large church in southern California. He was apprenticed to a gifted, respected pastor named Dr. Hart. These two men met two mornings a week for prayer and worked side-by-side every day. From Dr. Hart, Alex learned how to be a more organized administrator, a more competent counselor, and a more effective speaker.

Alex quickly blossomed into a vibrant, energetic preacher

with a unique message. Every time Alex preached—about one Sunday a month—attendance at Sunday morning worship went up.

At about the same time, Dr. Hart showed signs of increasing irritability and emotional distance from Alex. The help and advice he once offered so freely was now replaced by faultfinding. He began finding excuses to cancel their regular prayer time; and eventually, those prayer times ceased altogether.

It was clear to Alex that the mentoring relationship between himself and Dr. Hart had run its course and he would have to leave. He made up his mind to do so graciously, without bitterness and recrimination. Just a few weeks before he left to accept a position as pastor of a church in Florida, Alex sat down with Dr. Hart and recounted to him all the Christlike character qualities and important ministry skills he had learned from him. Alex thanked Dr. Hart for investing himself in his life. He graciously ignored the last six months of irritation and professional jealousy.

"What would have been the point?" Alex says today. "The mentoring relationship was over. I wasn't interested in parting shots, but in getting on with the next phase of my ministry. There have even been two or three times in the past few years when I've called him for advice about a problem or decision. On each occasion, he's been very gracious—just like the good old days."

Peter Hiett, a colleague on my staff, is a lot like Alex—a dynamic, gifted preacher. Although we have a great mutual respect for one another, Peter is technically the learner and I am his mentor. But I foresee a day when Peter will be one of the leading pastors in the country.

In the meantime, here's the question that confronts me as Peter's mentor: How will I feel if Sunday morning attendance increases whenever Peter steps into the pulpit? How will I feel if his message is received more positively than mine? Will I welcome that and rejoice with him? Or will I be jealous and resentful?

Whether a mentoring relationship succeeds or fails depends in large part on whether the mentor has an inner sense of security, contentment, and humility. There is no room in the mentoring process for jealousy and envy. When the mentor feels threatened by the learner, the mentoring process falters and dies.

As mentors, we not only welcome the growth and advancement of the learner, we pray for it and spend our lives coaching the learner toward that goal. The learner's success is our joy. As the learner surpasses us, we cheer him on and weep tears of joy.

We mentors perform a mystical and holy function, a priestly function. We initiate the next generation into ever deeper levels of emotional awareness and spiritual understanding. We do not merely *train* the learner; we actually impart to him or her our *blessing*. Our role as mentors is to anoint the next generation, to place the world in the hands of those who will succeed us.

Throughout those years I was growing up in my father's home, learning from him and watching his life, I was also being anointed and commissioned by him. I was receiving his blessing. He was preparing me to succeed him in the world. On the day I was ordained to the ministry, he placed a gift in my hands, a plaque that I kept for many years in my office. It read, in part,

> I do not ask that crowds throng the temple,
> That standing room be priced,
> I only ask that as I voice the message
> They may see Christ!
> I do not ask for earthly place or laurel
> Or of this world's distinctions any part;
> I only ask, when I have voiced the message
> That I may find my Savior's heart.

On the day Mike Flavin was ordained, I gave that plaque to him. One of the most rewarding experiences of my mentoring career has been to watch this learner become a mentor in his own right, to see his character grow and his gifts develop, to see God use him to make a powerful impact on many other young lives.

"When Ron gave me that plaque," Mike recalls, "it was like a blessing, the kind of blessing the older, wiser, more experienced men passed on to the younger men in biblical times. It meant a lot to me, because Ron's dad had given the plaque to him, and I knew it had always meant a lot to him. I keep that plaque in my office, and it reminds me of that special mentoring relationship. Ron and I live on opposite ends of the country now, but there's still a relationship, and a sense of being blessed and commissioned and sent out by my mentor. And that will last a lifetime."

Some mentoring relationships do last a lifetime. Others end with mentor and learner slowly drifting apart, as if one were on a departing ship and the other left standing on the shore. Still others end in a flash of lightning and a storm of thunder.

I have been blessed to experience few painful mentoring relationships. Almost all of the many mentors and learners I have befriended during my lifetime remain close friends.

Yet even if the mentoring relationship groans with strain and ends in pain, both the mentor and the learner can gain from the experience: Wisdom. Character growth. A deeper understanding of human motivations. Greater empathy. Greater mastery of the enigma of life.

As Walt Whitman said, we are trainers of athletes in a race for eternal glory. The champion who learns under us to shatter our own records and surpass our own faded glories pays us the greatest tribute a mentor can know. Even if the mentoring relationship eventually dies, that tribute will stand forever.

Chapter 12

MENTORING IN THE HOME

The mentor's most important task

WHAT CHILDREN REALLY WANT
FROM THEIR PARENTS

One of the most successful specialty card lines ever released by Hallmark is a series created to be given by parents to their children. Some of the cards bear the greeting "Have a good day!" and are designed to be placed under the child's morning bowl of Cheerios™. The idea is that dad and mom are both at work; the child is alone, getting ready for school. The child doesn't get a hug or a kiss, but he does get a nice Hallmark card. Other cards in the line include one to place on the child's pillow at night, which says, "I wish I could be here to tuck you in."

These greeting card messages are intended to be upbeat and cheerful. To me, they are deeply troubling. I grieve for the child that has a card instead of a bedtime story, an encourager in the stands at the Little League game, a hug before school.

Now, before going any further, I want to acknowledge some painful realities. You may be a single parent. Or both you and your spouse may need to work because the grocery bills and the rent just wouldn't get paid if you didn't. If you are in one of these two categories, I don't want to inflict any guilt on you. I want to commend you and applaud you. You're doing what you have to for the sake of your family. Unfortunately, we live in a society where it is becoming increasingly necessary for both parents to work just to meet the minimum costs of living.

Nor do I wish to suggest that a woman's place is only in the home. I believe women and men are equals in Christ and should be free to pursue careers as they feel led. Women should have equal treatment in the workplace in terms of pay and opportunity. I believe the apostle Paul affirmed the equality of women when he wrote, "There is neither Jew nor Greek, there is neither slave nor free, there is neither male nor female; for you are all one in Christ Jesus."[1] One reason I am proud to be a follower of Jesus Christ is that I believe he did more than any other person in human history to elevate the worth of women in human society.

Yet I know that there are many families in which both parents work not because of economic necessity but because they are obsessed with acquiring material possessions. Or because they are obsessed with success. Or because they are obsessed with security, with amassing huge investments, retirement funds, pensions, and the like. Or because they are workaholics and work is like a drug to them.

I've known many fathers and mothers who have worked themselves into exhaustion, some working fulltime plus moonlighting, while putting their children in daycare, all so they could "give the kids the things they deserve while they're growing up": the best schooling, the best clothes, the biggest house, the finest neighborhood, the shiniest toys. Yet, having visited with these children, I know that what they really want and need is *not* all the things money can buy, but *time*—time with their moms and dads.

"JUST" A MOTHER

Today, the traditional role of motherhood is under assault within our society. A cacophony of voices tell women that they cannot find meaning and fulfillment by being "just" a home-maker, "just" a mother. And I tire of hearing those voices.

Some time ago, I heard Tony Campolo tell the following story at a national youth workers convention. Campolo and his wife have three children. In their social circle, they are often invited to cocktail parties or mixers where they mingle with career women—attorneys, doctors, journalists, educators. Often Mrs. Campolo is asked by one of these professional women, "And what do you do?"

Her usual abashed and intimidated reply: "Me? Oh, I'm just a mother."

Soon she got tired of feeling defensive about being "just" a mother. One night, after one of these social gatherings, she sat down with a pencil and paper and wrote down what she thought was the job description of a mother. By the next cocktail party, she had it memorized. Now she was armed with a response for the "What do you do?" question.

Mrs. Campolo was not disappointed. She was introduced to a woman who looked like the cover of *Ms.* magazine. "And what do you do?" the woman asked.

"Well," said Mrs. Campolo as she gathered her verbal artillery, "I'm socializing two homo sapiens into the dominant values of the Christian belief system so that they might be agents for change, enabling the kingdom of God to triumph over the dying kingdoms of this world. Now . . . what do *you* do?"

"Oh, me?" said the other woman. "I'm just a doctor."

Mrs. Campolo is a mother who understands the crucial importance of mentoring in the home. She understands that the role of parent means a lot more than simply providing for a child's physical, emotional, and spiritual needs, as important as all that is. A biblical parent seeks to *mentor* his or her children, to give them a sense of vision and mission, to empower them to touch and influence other lives for Jesus Christ.

"THE CAPTAIN BITES HIS TONGUE . . ."

There was a time in the history of our culture when the mentoring process was just a natural aspect of family life. Parents, as a result of their life-style, naturally tended to invest themselves in the next generation.

Farmers raised their sons not only in the practical aspects of planting and harvest, but in the love of the earth and the lore of the seasons, in the value of hard work and loyalty to family. Fathers and sons worked closely in the family enterprise, as did mothers and daughters. Issues of faith, character, duty, and role images of manhood and womanhood were transmitted from parents to children not in any formal setting, but as the parents and children shared their lives together.

Our society has changed. The pace of our lives has quickened. Our families have become fragmented by activities, job pressures, and the lure of time-consuming entertainment media. These factors have not diminished the need for mentoring in the home; rather, they have made the need for the mentoring process all the more urgent.

Parents need to be there while that child is learning about life and making tough decisions, not to make the decision for the child, but to offer wisdom and experience. The hardest part of being a mentoring parent is learning to be there for our children without meddling in their hands-on experience of life. There is a saying in the Navy: "The captain bites his tongue until it bleeds." This expression refers to the way a ship's captain feels as he silently stands by, while allowing a junior officer to bring the ship alongside the dock for the first time. A wise mentoring parent will bite his tongue bloody many, many times before his or her child is an adult.

THE MYTH OF "QUALITY TIME"

One of the most profoundly important things my father did for me was that he inspired me with a sense of mission. He filled my youthful heart with a vision of the future, a realization that my life could touch other lives for Jesus Christ. He used to pray with my brother and me, saying, "Lord, help Paul and Ron to see that they can be leaders in their classrooms now, and that they can do great things for you in the years to come." I always carried my father's prayers within me, and now I pray that same prayer for my own children, Rachael and Nathan. As my dad did for me, I want to instill in them a sense of vision, a sense of who they are in Christ, and what they can do for Christ.

It takes *time*—the commitment of hours and hours to the task of parental mentoring—to build that kind of vision in our children. The tragedy of the 1990s is that fewer and fewer parents are willing to invest that kind of time in their children anymore. We whirl through our lives at such a hectic pace that our children simply get left in the dust.

I'm not talking here about secular parents, but about *Christian* parents. I'm talking about the well-meaning Christian businessman who wakes at 6:00 A.M., begins his long morning commute at 6:50 before the children are awake, works all day long in the city, and fights traffic all the way back to the suburbs, and then, instead of driving home, pulls into the church parking lot and attends yet another church committee meeting. By the time he gets home, his children are asleep. He has not seen them or talked to them all day.

I have spent many hours of my life in the presence of people who are spending their last hours on earth. It's a sobering experience. Many times, I've seen tears of anguish rolling down a dying man's cheeks, and I've listened to many dying regrets. But not once in all the years I've been in the pastoral profession have I ever heard a dying man say, "Ron, if I'd only spent more time at the office. What I really regret is that I didn't spend more time at work." Not once have I heard that.

But I have heard a lots of regrets like, "I wish I had spent more time with my wife. I wish I had spent more time with my kids. I wish I had spent more time with my friends."

Some of us parents wonder, "Why don't my children respond to my words of correction? Why don't my children respect my values? Why don't they respect and share my Christian faith?" While there are many ingredients which go into a strong parent-child relationship, some of which may be out of our control, it may be that we have not earned the right to be heard by our children. If we have not built a life-style of affirming, encouraging, and spending time with our children, we haven't genuinely been mentors in the home.

There is a pernicious myth in our culture, which has pervaded the Christian church, and it refuses to die. It is the myth of "quality time."

I recall with sadness a conversation I had a few years ago with a successful, ambitious businessman named Rodger. I had just shared with him some of the activities I had planned for the weekend with my two children, and what a joy it was for me to spend time with them.

"Well, Ron," Rodger replied, "that's fine for you and your family, I guess. But I think kids need space. They need time to do their own thing without Dad looking over their shoulders. I believe spending *quality* time is a lot more important than spending a big *quantity* of time with your kids."

I sensed that this "quality" versus "quantity" time argument was really an excuse he made to himself because he had spent virtually no time at all with his family.

Today Rodger is a very wealthy and successful man as the world counts wealth and success. But to me, his life is one of tragic failure and impoverishment, for today Rodger is completely estranged from his family. His children have nothing to do with him.

The amount of time we give our children is every bit as important as the quality of time. In fact, *without a large quantity of time, there is no quality time*. Like Rodger, you and I will only alienate and emotionally abuse our children until we cease looking at the quality/quantity issue as an either/or proposition. We must begin to see it as a both/and issue. We must give our children *both* quality *and* quantity time.

For some of us driven, task-oriented, Type-A people, that may mean we will have to give special thought, attention, and priority to making time to be with our families. We may have to schedule family time in our time management calendar. We may have to scratch off some of the business and social commitments we have made. We may have to ask other people to hold us accountable for creating both quality and quantity time with our families. If that's what it takes, then that's what we have to do. The most important people you and I as mentors need to invest ourselves in are the people under our own roof. Every other mentoring arena is secondary.

"I've been impressed," says Peter Hiett, "at how carefully and diligently Ron manages his time and his relationships, especially his family relationships, given how incredibly busy he is. From his example, I see it's possible to be in a highly visible position, with lots of people demanding your time, and still balance those demands with a rich family life and devotional life."

And Barb Cummelin, who has spent many hours in our home, says, "One of the most important things I've learned from both Ron and Shirley is the value of a family. I've known them since they were dating, and they've made me feel like a part of their family. I've watched how they interact with their kids. They always keep Monday night as a family night, with no interruptions, no matter how many demands people make

on Ron's time. He turns down a lot of speaking engagements
because he values his family so much. He knows how to make
his children feel special."

Not long ago, I took my son, Nathan, with me on a six-hour
car trip. Those were six good, quality hours. As we drove, we
talked together about all the things that interest him: school,
sports, and his favorite hobby, collecting baseball cards. Several hours into that journey, our conversation naturally turned
to our faith in Jesus Christ; to deeper issues of feelings and
fears and hopes, of what it means to be a twelve-year-old boy
and what it means to be a man in his early forties. We talked
about some of the hard things in life and some of the good
things.

Could such a quality conversation about feelings and faith
and the meaning of life have happened in a few moments of so-
called quality time? Real quality time needs a significant *quantity* of time to develop, ripen, and deepen. The groundwork of a
true parent-child friendship must be laid in time.

Are you and I taking a significant quantity of time to get to
know our children? The longer I live, as both a parent and a
counselor, the more I'm convinced that one of the greatest priv-
ileges and joys we can ever experience as parents and the greatest single contribution we can make in the lives of our children,
apart from leading them to Jesus Christ, is to get to *know* them.

YOUR CHILD'S UNIQUENESS

You cannot meet the emotional needs of a child you do not
know. You cannot meet the spiritual needs of a child you do not
know. You cannot properly train and mentor a child you do not
know. And you do not get to really know a child without spending a significant quantity of time with him or her.

Proverbs 22:6 says

> *Train up a child*
> *in the way he should go,*

> *And when he is old*
> *he will not depart from it.*

Does that simply mean that we should send our children to Sunday school, teach them the Ten Commandments, teach them how to say grace at mealtimes and how to pray at bedtime, send them to summer camp every year, and then, when that child grows up, he or she will still be a Christian? I've heard sermons and read books that interpret Proverbs 22:6 that way.

In the original Hebrew, however, that verse takes on a significantly different meaning. A more faithful rendering of Proverbs 22:6 might read, "Train up a child *according to his own unique characteristics,* and when he is older he will not depart from the faith." The Amplified Bible translates this verse, "Train up a child in keeping with his individual gifts, and when he is old he will not depart from the faith." In other words, we should adapt our efforts and methods of training our children so that they will help develop the unique traits and abilities which God has given them.

If you want to be a wise mentor to your child, then you must take the time to observe and understand your child, you must be sensitive to your child's unique characteristics, and you must adjust the training of *each* of your children to take those special differences into account.

I've seen many unwise parents (usually fathers) who refuse to heed the counsel of Proverbs 22:6, saying, "We're going to shape things up around here. Things are going to be done in the household the way I say." The child who is brought up under such a parent is repelled by this ultimatum and almost always rebels. Why? Because this father has violated the Word of God, which says that we are to be sensitive to the uniqueness of each child in our care.

Biblically, no parent has the right to say, "I will dictate absolutely to my child. This child is going to have my kind of character, values, abilities, and goals." Such a parent cannot authentically mentor his child. There are many subtle ways in which we ignore the advice of Proverbs 22:6 and violate the uniqueness of our children.

First, we ignore the advice of Proverbs 22:6 whenever we use a completely identical approach to rewarding, disciplining, helping, encouraging, and relating to each of our children. Certainly, we try to practice fairness, not favoritism, between our different children. But we must always remember that they *are* different children, with varying needs, abilities, desires, and goals. Our task as parental mentors is to encourage each child to find his or her unique gifts, to formulate his or her unique plans, to dream his or her own special dreams.

Second, we violate Proverbs 22:6 whenever we compare our children with their siblings or with other children. This is most grievous when we do so in front of them. It is an unwise, un-mentoring parent who would say, "Billy, why can't you just be neater and more organized, like your brother Tommy? Sally, why can't you just get the kind of grades your friend Gail gets? Larry, why can't you hit a baseball like your cousin Jason?" The more you try to make your child fit the mold of some other child, the more that child will rebel and think, "Mom, Dad, why can't you just take the time to get to know *me?* Why do I have to be something I'm not? Why do I have to be a carbon copy of some other kid? Why can't you just love me for who I am?"

MOUNTAINS TO CLIMB

Someone once said, "Children have more need of models than of critics." It's true. The wise mentoring parent knows that children need parents who are affirmers and examples, not evaluators and critics. The wise parent doesn't just demon-strate *appreciation* when the child does well, but continual, unconditional *affirmation,* regardless of the child's perfor-mance.

There is an enormous difference between appreciation and affirmation. We *appreciate* what a person *does*. We *affirm* who a person *is*. If all we ever express to our children is appreciation when they have performed well, then they will conclude, consciously or unconsciously, that they are only loved for their achievements and good behavior. This leads to self-doubt and emotional insecurity. Certainly we want to praise and encourage our children when they achieve and succeed. But it is only when we move beyond conditional appreciation to genuine affirmation, whether they are struggling or succeeding, that our children will feel unconditionally loved and emotionally secure.

Affirmation is at the root of encouragement. Paul counsels us as mentors in the home, "Do not provoke your children, lest they become discouraged."[2] We are commanded to encourage and build up our children. Tragically, numerous studies suggest that the typical American parent offers far more criticism than affirmation to his or her children.

But it doesn't have to be that way. The family of Rick Leavenworth understood this fact.

When Rick was six years old, he was injured in an accident that severed his spinal cord, rendering his legs useless. Yet, because he had parents who affirmed and encouraged him, Rick Leavenworth grew up believing he could conquer many challenges that most non-handicapped people would be afraid to attempt.

One of the challenges Rick Leavenworth took on was the rugged outdoor sport of mountain climbing. His proudest accomplishment: conquering a 13,000-foot mountain with just his wheelchair, his determination, and the message his parents had repeatedly reinforced within him: "You can do it! We believe in you!" Rick Leavenworth's parents looked at their son and saw him in his uniqueness, with both his limitations and his strengths. They raised him to believe he could climb mountains.

You and I as parents need to be aware that our kids have a lot of rugged mountains to climb. For them, the challenges may not be physical. Instead, they may face the challenge of taking a moral stand against overwhelming peer pressure; or the challenge of taking a stand for Jesus Christ on their campus; or the challenge of living out a life-style of integrity while all their friends practice a life-style without values or limits. As our kids climb those mountains, they need specific encouragement and affirmation from their parents. They need to hear us telling them, "I'm on your side, not on your back."

Moreover, they need someone to teach them all the ingredients, great and small, that add up to a happy, responsible, meaningful adult life. At different stages in your child's life you will be called upon to mentor them, both by your words and the quality of your life, in

- accepting responsibility for mistakes;
- voting and taking civic responsibility;
- working hard and being diligent;
- understanding the place of sex in human relations;
- taking courageous moral stands;
- becoming a young man or woman of God;
- taking up the life-and-death responsibility of driving a car;
- handling money—spending and investing it wisely, tithing and giving sacrificially to God, and even balancing a checkbook.

These are things that generally are not taught at all or are not taught well in schools. These are among the many things you will have to pass on to your children by the mentoring process.

THE PROBLEM WITH CARBON PAPER

In the movie *Parenthood*, Steve Martin portrayed a loving but compulsive, neurotic father. At one point in the film, this father expresses his exasperation over the fact that his nine-year-old boy must go into psychological counseling. Turning to his wife, he says, "Why is our son so *compulsive?!*"

The silent look his wife returns is all the answer he needs. His son is compulsive because he himself is so compulsive.

He sighs, and then with deep sincerity, holding his hands in front of him as if cradling a newborn infant, he says, "You know, when your baby is born, he seems so perfect. You haven't made any mistakes yet. And then that baby grows up to be . . . to be just like *me*."

For good or ill, that's what parenthood is all about.

There is an invisible sheet of carbon paper between a parent and a child, isn't there? Mentoring in the home has to do with the kind of impression we allow to pass through that invisible sheet of carbon paper to our children. With every new day, we put another trace, another mark on the new generation that is growing up under our roof. It's only natural that we want to stamp our child only with that part of ourselves that is good, healthy, positive, happy.

But it doesn't work that way, does it? There's no filtering process, no way of screening out the impurities, so that only the good, the holy, and the healthy get through. The carbon paper between ourselves and our children is not selective. It simply transfers the image of who we are, warts, sins, mistakes, and all.

So often the very traits we disliked in our parents and now detest in ourselves soon begin to emerge in our children: The impatient nature. The critical spirit. The profane tongue. The procrastinating temperament. The manipulative guile. The violent temper. The lust for possessions and power. All these things are passed on from parent to child, even though the parent may try to talk and plead and punish those traits out of the child.

Why? Because the reality of who we are shouts louder than our words.

If we could give any present to our children at their next
birthday, many of us would give to them the gift of a spiritual
eraser with which they could rub out all the destructive character traits they absorbed from us. But there is no spiritual eraser.

So what's the answer?

How do we become nurturing spiritual mentors to our children despite the fact that we are fallible human beings, filled
with sin, bad habits, and negative character traits we ourselves
have inherited from the generation before us?

We must find a way to break the cycle.

In my family, both my mother and my father were anxiety-
prone. My brother Paul and I were both anxiety-prone from
childhood on into adulthood. So the question that confronts me
as a mentor in the most important arena of all is, Will my children Rachael and Nathan grow to be as prone to anxiety and
worry as I am? Or will I make the decision to break that cycle?
Will I begin to do all I can in partnership with God to check
and reverse this multigenerational character flaw that exists in
our family?

The particular issue, the particular character flaw, that runs
through your family and which now threatens the spiritual
well-being of your children may be far different from the ones I
am dealing with, but the principle is the same. You must decide
to break the cycle.

Remember the mentoring advice of Thomas Carlyle: "Be
what you would have your pupils be." In the home, our pupils
are our children. If you want to have children who are healthy
and happy and well-adjusted, then you will have to take a close
look at your own life and ask yourself, "Am I happy? Are my
relationships healthy? Do I have a good marriage, filled with
love and respect between myself and my spouse?"

If not, then you need to take positive action to break the
cycle. You need to talk honestly with your mate about your
relationship. You may also need to talk to a close friend or a

support group, so that you will have someone praying for you and holding you accountable to take steps toward healing in your marriage relationship. You may even need to go with your spouse to a counselor. Whatever it takes to become a whole person with a whole marriage, *that* is what you must do to break the cycle.

If you want to have children of integrity and honesty, then you will have to become a person of integrity and honesty yourself. That means if the store clerk gives you change for a $20 bill when you know you gave that clerk a $10 bill, you don't quietly pocket that extra money. You say, "Excuse me, but you gave me too much change." And that means you don't slip your thirteen-year-old child into the theater or the restaurant when you see a sign that says, "Children 12 and Under—Half Price," even if your child could easily pass for an eleven-year-old. And that means you don't drive fifteen miles over the speed limit because you're late getting your child to school.

If you want children who pray, who love the Lord Jesus, and who have good moral values, then you will have to become exactly the kind of person you want them to be. That means you must begin to pray with your children not just at bedtime, but in those joyful times when your children have something they want to thank God for, and in those tough times when your children need to ask for God's help or forgiveness. It also means you are going to have to become a person who demonstrates love for God, love for other Christians, love for God's Word, and a love for doing what is right.

Your children are watching the way you live much more closely than they are listening to the words you say. If you want a prescription for disaster in raising your children, I can think of nothing more destructive than communicating to them, "Do as I say and not as I do."

"But, Ron," you may protest, "I'm not perfect! I make mistakes! Lots of them! Big ones, too! As hard as I try to do what's right, I'm still afraid I'm going to ruin my kids with my own bad example! Isn't there any hope for a sinning, fallible, neurotic parent like me?"

Yes, there's hope. For even though it's impossible to live a perfect life before our children, we can still live earnestly, honestly, transparently, with an intense passion for godliness. *That* is what our children want to see in us: not a fraudulent facade of perfection, but an authentic life, lived in the dust and sweat and tears of our humanity.

Our children don't want to have parents who never fail; they want parents who pick themselves up and try again. Our children don't want parents who never sin; they want parents who model a life-style of forgiving and being forgiven. Our children don't want parents without hurts and frailties and character flaws; they want parents who confess their inadequacies and express their commitment to growth, to sanctification, to becoming more and more like Christ.

That is what our children want us to be like as mentors in the home. And when you think about it, that's also what we want our children to be like as they grow up.

When our goal ceases to be perfection, but rather a commitment to growth, then we no longer have to fear that invisible sheet of carbon paper between ourselves and our children.

WINNERS OR LOSERS?

When I was about eight or nine years old, I joined a Little League baseball team with some of my friends. Practice was held at a baseball diamond in the public park of my hometown. I had never played much baseball before. My dad never played baseball, so he never had the opportunity to teach me the game. I didn't know the proper way to grip a bat, throw a ball, catch a fly, or snag a grounder.

I remember going through the first practice, fumbling fly after fly, missing one grounder after another. About two-thirds of the way through the practice, the coach said to all the boys,

"I want all of you except Ron to go sit on the bleachers. I'm going to teach Ron how to field some grounders."

There I was, singled out in front of all my peers on a hot, humid day, while the coach hit grounder after grounder in my direction. They went between my legs or bounced off my shoe or my glove. He would hit pop flies that would drop to my left or my right. I tried. I tried until my heart felt like bursting. I just couldn't get it.

I was humiliated in front of my friends.

The ordeal lasted about half an hour. Finally, I just gave up and walked away in tears. I was ashamed. To this day, I run, I play basketball, I play touch football. But I never play baseball, even at the church picnic or the staff softball games in the park.

The coach wasn't trying to be cruel. He was trying to help me, to give me individual attention. But what he accomplished was to make me feel like a loser in front of my friends.

Tragically, many of us parents unwittingly do the same thing to our children. We don't mean to be cruel. We don't mean to make our children feel like losers when we scold them for that disappointing grade or compare them to other children or try to squeeze their unique temperament into the mold of our own personality. Yet that's exactly what we do.

Ultimately, our goal is to empower our children to make a difference for Jesus Christ in this world. That means we encourage them to have the kind of faith in God and confidence in themselves that enables them to positively go out and achieve great things for God.

Our job, in short, is to enable our children to see themselves as *winners*.

How do we help our kids to grow up feeling like winners? How do we discover the unique characteristics of our children so that we can affirm those traits and channel them for the sake of their emotional health and happiness and for furtherance of the kingdom of God? Again, the wise mentoring parent turns to the Scriptures for the answer. Proverbs 20:11–12 says "a child is known by his deeds. . . . The hearing ear and the seeing eye, the LORD has made both of them."

A child makes himself or herself known by his or her actions, which we must observe with a hearing ear and a seeing eye. Are we praying for sensitivity, for opportunities to get to know our children in deeper and more meaningful ways? Do we intentionally, determinedly *study* our children, so that we can adapt our efforts to train, discipline, and encourage each child in a way that matches his or her unique characteristics?

God's book of ancient wisdom is just as potent and applicable in the 1990s as it ever was: "Train up a child in the way he should go, and when he is old he will not depart from it." Brought down to its essentials, that is the job description of every biblical mentoring parent.

Chapter 13

HOW TO LIVE FOREVER
Pouring our lives into others

THE DOCTOR DIED, BUT THE PATIENT LIVED

Boris Kornfeld was a Russian Jew imprisoned in one of Stalin's notorious gulags. Though trained as a doctor, Kornfeld's medical skills were largely wasted in a place where human life was a cheap and degraded commodity. Assigned a position in the prison hospital, most of the "medicine" he was allowed to practice involved the signing of false medical documents which allowed the guards to place prisoners in solitary torture chambers. The documents stated that the prisoners were physically strong enough to endure the punishment; Kornfeld knew those men would die.

Kornfeld despised Christianity. He had grown up embracing communism and hating the Christian religion of the Czars, who had persecuted Russian Jews. Yet, though he had always been a committed communist, Kornfeld had been accused of some crime against the State and was now condemned to spend the rest of his life in prison. Now, disillusioned and betrayed by his atheist "religion" called communism, Kornfeld was a man without hope or faith.

While in prison, he encountered a fellow prisoner who told him about a Jewish Messiah who had come many centuries before to fulfill the promises God made to Israel. The man told Kornfeld that this Jesus had come to the Jews first, and now called all of mankind to himself. As the other prisoner recited the Lord's Prayer to him, Kornfeld found himself strangely moved and attracted to this Christian message he had previously rejected.

Eventually, Kornfeld's Christian friend was taken away to an unknown fate. Yet the gospel message continued to creep slowly into Boris Kornfeld's heart. Over a period of months, Kornfeld began to feel changed and warmed. The hatred he felt toward the cruel guards and officers began to melt. His despair turned to hope.

Yet, his conscience troubled him. Kornfeld knew he could no longer sign the false documents and be a party to sending his fellow prisoners to their deaths. He knew he couldn't change the fate of the doomed men. But he also knew he could no longer endure that stain on his soul. So he refused to sign.

It was around this time that he caught an orderly stealing food from a dying man in the prison hospital. Before his conversion, Kornfeld would have turned a blind eye to the incident. Now, with a Christian sense of right and wrong, he knew he had to report the orderly's actions to the prison officials, even though the orderlies were known to take revenge against "stoolies." The orderly received three days in the punishment block, then was released.

A few days later, Kornfeld was in the hospital, checking on patients, when he came upon a man who had just had an operation for intestinal cancer. Even though the patient was groggy and incoherent from the anesthetic, Kornfeld began to talk to him. He told the patient about the change that had come over his heart after someone shared the gospel with him. He shared about the forgiveness and hope he felt in his heart, despite the cruelty and misery of the gulag. Even in his anesthetic fog, the patient clung to Kornfeld's words until he finally fell asleep.

Hours later, when the patient awoke, the man in the next bed told him the news that was being whispered all over the hospital: Dr. Kornfeld was dead. During the night, someone had crushed his skull with a mallet while he lay sleeping.

The patient was stricken with grief. But he was also filled with the conviction that Jesus was now alive within himself, that the life and faith that had been inside of Boris Kornfeld had somehow been transferred into his own being. The doctor had died, but the patient lived.

The patient's name was Alexander Solzhenitsyn.

Kornfeld had performed a beautiful act of "heart to heart resuscitation," pouring the last remaining drops of his life into Solzhenitsyn. Kornfeld never knew the powerful effect his witness had, not only on Solzhenitsyn, but through him, upon the entire world.

In the last hours of his life, Boris Kornfeld lived the life-style of a mentor.

A mentor is one who pours his life *into* others, and is willing even to pour his life out *for* others. Dietrich Bonhoeffer said that a righteous person is one who lives for the next generation. What a tremendous tribute, what a fitting epitaph that would be for you and me at the end of our lives: "He lived for the next generation." "She lived for the next generation."

Brought down to its essentials, mentoring is the process of investing our lives in those who come after us, beginning with our own children, and spreading out to all those men, women, and young people God brings into our lives.

Do you want immortality? Do you want to live forever? Do you want to live on even after your death? Then, beginning today, live the life-style of a mentor.

Boris Kornfeld will live forever. My father and my brother will live forever. I know I will live forever too. So can you.

THE IMMORTAL MENTOR

We live on after our death in only *two* ways: First, we live on in eternity with Jesus. Second, we live on in the lives of those whom we have mentored.

A man named Walt intuitively understood the mentoring principle. He had an ambition to start a Sunday school class for the kids in his neighborhood. So he started with one boy he found playing marbles on the sidewalk. "Son," he said, "I'd like you to come to a Sunday school class with me."

The boy turned his grimy face up at Walt and sneered, "No way, mister! You won't catch me going to any Sunday school!"

"Well, we'll see," Walt said. "Say, that's a mighty pretty shooter you have there. And look at all those aggies and puries! I remember when I was a boy, walking around with a bag full of marbles rattling in my pocket. Yes sir, there's no finer feeling than having a pocketful of marbles, is there?"

"I guess not," the boy said dubiously.

"Mind if I shoot a few, son?"

"Well, no, go ahead, mister." The boy was frankly perplexed by this strange grown up who admired his marbles and got down on his knees on the sidewalk and began shooting like an expert.

They played several games of marbles together, right there on the sidewalk. Finally, the boy grinned at Walt and said, "Say, mister, you're okay. Now, where was this Sunday school you wanted me to go to?"

So Walt and his young friend went through the neighborhood and gathered twelve more boys and started a Sunday school class. Over the ensuing weeks, Walt gave himself sacrificially to those thirteen boys. They studied the Bible together, they went on hikes together, they played marbles and stickball together.

As Walt continued to pour himself into those boys, a strong bond of friendship grew between them. Eventually, a time came when the hearts of those boys were softened and prepared soil for the seed of the gospel. Walt shared with them the good news of a man named Jesus, who died for their sins, and who rose again and wanted to live his life through them. Those boys eagerly responded. They accepted Jesus into their hearts. Their lives were changed forever.

Today, those boys have grown to manhood. Eleven of the thirteen are in fulltime vocational service for Jesus Christ. The first boy, the one Walt encountered on the sidewalk playing marbles, grew to become the chairman of the Center for Christian Leadership and a distinguished professor at Dallas Theological Seminary. A renowned author and speaker and a mentor in his own right to hundreds of students, his name is Howard Hendricks.

Walt's body was laid to rest a few years ago. But Walt isn't really gone. He lives on in eternity. And he lives on in the lives of the thirteen individuals he mentored. And he will continue to live on in the lives of all the people who will in turn be mentored by them.

In addition to the assurance of eternity with Jesus, it is a great assurance to know that a part of us goes on living in the people we mentor. Whenever I spend time with someone who has been profoundly influenced by the life of my father or my brother, I experience a feeling of refreshment and joy. It's as if I am actually in the presence of that departed loved one and, in a very real sense, I *am*.

A part of my brother lives on in the scores of lives he affected as a teacher, coach, and mentor in Colorado and across the country. A part of my father lives on in the scores of lives he touched and imprinted during his twenty-five years as a pastor in Iowa.

It seems every time I go back to my hometown of Clarinda, Iowa, people tell me how much they loved my dad and how they fondly recall the things he did to help people in the church and the community. But more than that, I can see that something of the Christlikeness of my father has become embedded in the lives of these people, making them more like Christ.

I remember one woman named Ruth saying to me, "Ron, after I lost my own father, I really needed a spiritual father. Your dad was always there to give me guidance when I was a newlywed. I had a lot of growing up to do during those years, but your dad counseled me and prayed with me and helped me be God's person in my marriage and with my children."

Just think of it: You and I can be immortal, not only in eternity, but here on earth. Even after your death, you can reach out and touch unborn generations through the life of someone you have mentored. You can continue to impact countless lives, long after you have gone to be with the Lord, because you have lived the lifestyle of a mentor.

THE MASTER MENTOR LIVES ON

Jesus, the Master Mentor, is our example in life and in death. After pouring his life into the lives of the Twelve, he was ready and willing to pour out his own life on the cross. Because Jesus knew he would live on in two ways, he was confident his story wouldn't end when he was taken to a hill and executed. He knew he would live on through those he mentored and through the millions of spiritual descendants of those he mentored.

Today, Jesus lives on in you and me. And he lives on in eternity, Lord of Lords and King of Kings. Our goal in life is to identify with him, to become like him, in both life and death.

As we examine his life and emulate his life, we see that Jesus attracted the Twelve to himself. He lived and walked among them, taught them by his word and example, encouraged them, and challenged them. He also mentored Mary and Martha, the sisters of Lazarus. He mentored a deeply religious man named Nicodemus and taught him a better way. He mentored ignorant fishermen and corrupt tax collectors and radical extremists. All these lives, and many more, he touched and transformed during his short lifetime. He molded and shaped this diverse group of people into a powerful, cohesive force which ultimately changed the world.

Mentoring is the primary method Jesus chose to spread the faith he founded, and it is the primary method by which Christianity has been propagated from generation to generation and around the world for the past two thousands years. As we examine the life and life-style of Jesus, we find that even though he preached and healed among the masses, he spent a vastly greater portion of his time in an intense relationship with just twelve individuals.

Jesus never ruled a nation or led an army or wrote a book. Yet his message has been spread from those ancient Judean hillsides to the farthest reaches of this computer-age world. It didn't happen because Jesus was a master of mass communication techniques or management skills or leadership training, but because he was a mentor. He invested his message in *people*.

CRUNCHING THE NUMBERS

Our generation is mesmerized by big numbers. We've bought the notion that if we just pump enough print media, broadcast media, and seminar speakers into the world, the world will listen and be changed. The problem with this scenario is that mass communication techniques make a comparatively shallow imprint and only influence lives in batches of a hundred, a thousand, or a million at a time.

Mentoring, however, operates on the principle of exponential growth. Initially, the mentoring process impacts only a few people, but it impacts them at a very deep level. And while it yields deceptively small returns at the outset, it quickly mushrooms as the yield compounds, multiplies, and factors itself.

There is an ancient tale that illustrates the amazing growth potential of exponential growth.

Once there was a king who desired to have a statue of himself for the courtyard of his castle. He asked his advisors for the name of the most gifted sculptor in the world. When they gave him the name of a world-renowned artist from a far country, the king sent for him. Several weeks later, the artist arrived at the castle and was brought before the king, who was sitting across a table from the court bishop, engaged in a game of chess.

"I'm sorry to interrupt your game, your majesty," said the artist, "but I came as soon as I received your summons. How may I be of service to your highness?"

"I would like to commission you," said the king, "to carve my likeness in marble, to stand on a pedestal in the courtyard."

"It will take time, your majesty," answered the sculptor. "And it will cost a great deal of gold."

"How much time?" the king inquired warily. "And how much gold?"

"The statue will take sixty-four days to complete," said the artist. "And the fee for my services is one thousand gold pieces per day."

"Sixty-four thousand gold pieces!" the king exploded. "Preposterous!"

"The king finds my fee excessive?" the artist said with a patient smile. "Then perhaps I can suggest a fee schedule more to the king's liking. You see the chessboard before you? There are sixty-four squares on that board, one of every day of my task. All I ask is that tomorrow as I begin my work, you place one copper penny on the first square. On the second day of my labor, double my wages and place two pennies on the second square. On the third day, four pennies on the third square. On the fourth day, eight pennies. On the fifth day, sixteen pennies. Continue doubling my wages until the statue is completed and every square on the board is filled. That shall be my fee."

The king smiled, inwardly congratulating himself for having secured the artist's services for mere pennies a day. "Agreed," he said.

"Good," the sculptor said. "Let us consider the bargain sealed at the moment I set my chisel to stone, tomorrow morning."

The next day, the king stood by a window, watching as the artist positioned a large marble block in the courtyard. Just then, the chancellor of the exchequer entered the chamber and cleared his throat. "I have come as you commanded, sire," said the chancellor, "and I have brought the copper penny you ordered, though I must confess I am at a loss to understand why—"

"Place it on the first square of the chessboard," said the king, chuckling smugly. "That penny represents an entire day's wages for that fool of a sculptor."

The chancellor blinked in befuddlement. "Sire?"

The king laughed heartily, then explained the sculptor's fee schedule to the chancellor. The chancellor looked at the chessboard and performed several rapid mental calculations. Then he turned very white. "Sire, stop that man!"

"Are you mad?" the king growled.

"Stop him before he sets chisel to stone or you will bankrupt the realm! Look!" The chancellor pointed to the first row of eight squares. "Here is the penny in the first square. Now double that amount, square by square: 2, 4, 8, 16, 32, 64, 128 pennies per day. Second row: 256, 516, 1,024, 2,048, 4,096, 8,192, 16,384, 32,768 pennies per day. By the end of the third row, 8,388,608 pennies per day. By the end of the fourth row, over two billion pennies per day—that's more than two million pieces of gold! Fifth row, over half a trillion pennies a day. The royal exchequer is long since bankrupt and there are still three rows to go!"

"Enough!" the king shrieked, his face ashen. Turning about, he raced out of the chamber, down the stairs, and into the courtyard. The sculptor stood with his hammer and chisel poised to strike the first chip from the marble block. "Stop!" cried the king. "I will pay your original price!"

"Agreed," the sculptor said, smirking with satisfaction. "One thousand gold pieces per day." He then proceeded to carve the statue.

The point of the story is plain. Imagine that those pennies on the chessboard are not coins but *people*. One person mentors another; now there are two. Those two each mentor another; now there are four. Soon there are eight, then sixteen, and on and on and on.

As any computer wizard will tell you, all you have to do is "crunch the numbers" and it's easy to see why Jesus, the Master Mentor, chose to invest so much of himself in a few people. It's easy to see why more time spent with fewer people really does equal greater lasting impact for God. And it's easy to see why the mentoring life-style spells immortality for you and me.

There is a miraculous kind of joy and wonder that comes with knowing that when you invest something of yourself in another person, that *something* goes on, it multiplies, it spreads around the world and continues through time. One of the greatest joys of my life is seeing how the people I mentored ten, fifteen, or twenty years ago are now mentoring a new generation. One of these is Barb Cummelin.

"Nowadays," says Barb, "I'm involved in mentoring relationships with junior high and high school kids at church. People ask me, 'Why do you want to work with church kids after dealing with college students all day long?' But I really love that age group. My mentoring relationship with Ron meant so much to me, and I want to give that back to other young people.

"There are three girls I mentored in Iowa before I moved to Seattle. We keep in touch constantly. When one of them was injured in an accident, the other girls called me right away and said, 'Sarah's in the hospital.' They send me tapes and letters telling me about their schoolwork, how they're growing in their faith, what boys they're interested in this week. I care about what's happening in their lives. And part of the reason, I believe, is that someone took that kind of interest in my own life."

Not long ago, I heard Bob Kraning, associate pastor at the First Evangelical Free Church of Fullerton, speak these words at Forest Home, a Christian conference center in southern California:

> The ultimate success of my life will not be judged
> by the number of those who admire me for my ac-
> complishments, but by the number of those who
> attribute their wholeness to my love for them—by
> the number of those who have seen their true
> beauty and worth in my eyes.

Don't you want to be a success by the standards Bob Kraning outlines? Don't you want to be that eternal kind of success, one whose life is summed up not by a tally of wealth accumulated or monuments erected, but in the number of lives touched, changed, and made whole? I do. With all my heart, I do.

THE HEART OF A MENTOR

In 1 Timothy 3 and Titus 1, the apostle Paul listed the qualities and qualifications for people who would occupy positions of leadership and influence in the church. I believe these lists are just as applicable to the role of mentor as to other positions of influence, such as pastor or elder. Here is my own paraphrase of Paul's qualifications for a biblical mentor:

1. A mentor must be well-established in the Christian faith, not a recent convert.
2. A mentor must be a person of good reputation and above reproach.
3. A mentor must be faithful to his or her spouse.
4. A mentor must be level-headed and self-controlled, not controlled by bad habits or addictions.
5. A mentor must be honest and genuine.

6. A mentor must love what is good, upright, and holy.
7. A mentor must be biblically literate, daily studying and holding firmly the truths of Scripture.
8. A mentor must be able to teach others.
9. A mentor must be hospitable, ready to welcome both friends and strangers.
10. A mentor must have a gentle and gracious spirit, not given to violent outbursts of anger, not quarrelsome.
11. A mentor must not be a lover of money and material possessions.
12. A mentor must be a mentor in the home *first;* that is, a mentor must prove that he or she can nurture, love, teach, train, and counsel his or her own children before attempting to be an example to others.

The heart of a mentor is described for us in 1 Thessalonians 2:8, where the apostle Paul told his friends in Thessalonica that he was willing to share with them not only the Gospel, but his very life. A man named James Sullivan attempted to be a mentor to young people while lacking a mentor's heart. He was willing to share the Gospel, but he was not willing to share his own life.

Sullivan later described himself as "an achievement-oriented Christian"—driven, task-oriented, Type-A personality. Because of his achievement-oriented personality, he was able to build the largest Young Life Club in the United States. He was self-reliant and self-sufficient—or so he thought until his self-contained life-style tore his family apart.

His wife, Carolyn, had a complete emotional breakdown because she felt completely alone and abandoned in their marriage relationship. Sullivan was forced to examine the results of his achievement-oriented life-style when he took his wife to the hospital and checked her into the psychiatric ward.

Sullivan had always thought his family would only love him if he kept up a front of invincibility. After leaving her in the hospital, he went back to his car where the children waited. As he climbed into the car, he began to weep. Big tears of inner pain rolled down his cheeks. He tried to hide those tears from his children, but they noticed. And to his surprise, they loved him even more because of his vulnerability.

During the next few months, Sullivan—who had always given himself to others—suddenly had to learn how to receive from others. It was a humbling experience. Friends paid for his wife's hospitalization because the Sullivans couldn't afford it. Friends brought meals to their home, cleaned the bathroom, washed the dishes, and vacuumed the carpets.

"I had never shared my life with anyone else," he later recalled, "not even my wife and children. I always thought you were adequate if you could love other people, but you were inadequate if you let other people love you."

While trying to be a mentor to hundreds of young people outside his home, Sullivan had failed to be a mentor to his own family. Fortunately, he realized in time how much he needed the love of his wife and children and how much he needed other Christians. Most important of all, he realized how much he needed to share his life with other people.

Today, James Sullivan is a mentor in the truest sense of the word. In his home and in his mentoring relationships, he honestly reveals not only his strengths and his abilities, but his hurts, his frailties, and his feelings.

That's what it means to share your life with others. That's what it means to be a mentor.

In his book *Who Switched the Price Tags?*, Anthony Campolo related the words of the pastor of a black Baptist church, speaking to a group of college students in his congregation. Campolo wrote,

"Children," he said, "you're going to *die!* . . . One of these days, they're going to take you out to the cemetery, drop you in a hole, throw some dirt on your face, and go back to the church and eat potato salad.

"When you were born," he said, "you alone were crying and everybody else was happy. The important question I want to ask is this: When you die are you alone going to be happy, leaving everybody else crying? The answer depends on whether you live to get titles or you live to get testimonies. When they lay you in the grave, are people going to stand around reciting the fancy titles you earned, or are they going to stand around giving testimonies of the good things you did for them? . . . Will you leave behind just a newspaper column telling people how important you were, or will you leave crying people who give testimonies of how they've lost the best friend they ever had?

"There's nothing wrong with titles. Titles are good things to have. But if it ever comes down to a choice between a title or a testimony—go for the testimony."[1]

As mentors, we are going for the testimony. When we choose to invest our lives in others, we embark on the most exciting and rewarding adventure imaginable.

We are involved in a process that takes place in hidden places, in quiet moments. Yet with time, it multiplies and compounds, transforming lives, communities, nations, and the world itself.

You and I will live forever. Even in death, we mentors are immortal. We have the rare privilege of living on, not only in eternity with Jesus, but in the lives of all those people we impact for Jesus.

There is no better way to live than to live forever as a mentor.

NOTES

Chapter One: Living for the Next Generation

1. Proverbs 27:17 NIV.
2. Sergius C. Lorit, *The Last Days of Maximilian Kolbe* (New York: New City Press, 1968), 27.
3. *Ibid.*, 29.
4. *Ibid.*, 47.

Chapter Two: A Learner's Notebook

1. Ruth 1:16.
2. Titus 2:3–5.
3. Charles R. Swindoll, *Dropping Your Guard* (Waco, TX: Word Books, 1983), 171.
4. Bruce Larson, *There's a Lot More to Health Than Not Being Sick* (Waco, TX: Words Books, 1981), 61.

Chapter Three: Becoming a Mentor

1. 1 John 1:1.
2. Quoted in *Discipleship Journal,* Issue 41 (1987), 25.
3. *Ibid.*
4. Quoted in *Discipleship Journal,* Issue 32 (1985), 26.
5. John 13:15.

Chapter Four: Tender Toughness

1. 1 Thessalonians 2:7.
2. 2 Corinthians 2:4.
3. 2 Timothy 1:3–4; 4:9.

Chapter Five: The Mentor and Failure

1. Thomas J. Peters and Robert H. Waterman, Jr., *In Search of Excellence: Lessons from America's Best-Run Companies* (New York: Harper & Row, 1982), 223.
2. Charles R. Swindoll, *Improving Your Serve* (Waco, TX: Word Books, 1981), 165.
3. Stephen D. Shores, *Discipleship Journal,* Issue 28 (1985), 20.

Chapter Six: Integrity

1. 1 Kings 9:4–7.
2. Ron Willingham, *Integrity Selling* (Garden City, NY: Doubleday & Co., 1987), 87.

Chapter Seven: Devotion

1. For many of the ideas in this chapter, I am deeply indebted to two books, *Strengthening Your Grip* by Charles Swindoll (Word Books, 1982) and *The Gospel of Matthew* by William Barclay (Big Island, VA: St. Andrew Press, 1956).
2. Matthew 23:14.
3. Matthew 6:7.
4. Mark 14:36.
5. Romans 8:15; Galatians 4:6.

Chapter Eight: Wisdom

1. Matthew 19:24.
2. Daniel 2:20–21.
3. Psalm 19:7.
4. James 1:5.
5. Kenneth Blanchard and Norman Vincent Peale, *The Power of Ethical Management* (New York: William Morrow, 1988), 18–24.
6. Colossians 4:5.
7. 1 Corinthians 10:23.
8. Romans 14:21.
9. 1 Corinthians 10:24.

Chapter Nine: Motivation

1. Lee Iacocca with William Novak, *Iacocca: An Autobiography* (New York: Bantam Books, 1984), 34–36.
2. Nehemiah 2:17.
3. Matthew 16:24–25.
4. Thomas J. Peters and Robert H. Waterman, Jr., *In Search of Excellence: Lessons from America's Best-Run Companies* (New York: Harper & Row, 1982), 57.
5. Acts 11:24.
6. 2 Timothy 4:11.
7. Romans 12:15.
8. John 14:12.

Chapter Ten: Perseverance

1. 2 Timothy 3:11.
2. See 1 Timothy 1:20 and 2 Timothy 4:14.
3. 3 John 10.
4. Nehemiah 4:2–3.
5. Jerry Cook with Stanley C. Baldwin, *Love, Acceptance & Forgiveness* (Ventura, CA: Regal Books, 1979), 19.

6. 1 Samuel 17:47.
7. 2 Corinthians 4:8–9.

Chapter Twelve: Mentoring in the Home
1. Galatians 3:28.
2. Colossians 3:21.

Chapter Thirteen: How to Live Forever
1. Anthony Campolo, *Who Switched the Price Tags?* (Waco, TX: Word Books, 1986), 58–59.

ACKNOWLEDGMENTS

A number of my friends have contributed to the process of publishing *Mentoring: The Strategy of the Master,* and I want to express my deep gratitude to each one.

My friend and brother in Christ, Jim Denney, has researched, refined, developed, and edited the material for this book, as in all seven of our previous books. His diligent effort and his craftsmanship as a writer are evident in every line.

Helen McKinney, my gifted administrative assistant and dear friend, has carefully critiqued each chapter of this book and has been a constant source of encouragement to me, to my co-author Jim Denney, and to our friends at Thomas Nelson Publishers. Helen is a special gift of God's grace to me and my ministry.

This book would not exist were it not for my editor at Thomas Nelson Publishers, Janet Thoma. The idea for this project grew out of many discussions we had together, and she envisioned, catalyzed, nurtured, and coaxed into being many of the concepts of this book. Her commitment to excellence is exceeded only by her commitment to Jesus Christ. Janet is a joy to work with.

Joan Callahan, a special sister in Christ, has spent many hours organizing and cataloging material from my speaking so that it could be more readily adapted in written form.

I'm also grateful to those special friends whose names appear throughout this book, and who graciously consented to be interviewed regarding the mentoring relationships we have shared together. Their observations, so vulnerably and honestly offered, have given this book a meaningful dimension it would not have otherwise had.

Most of all, I am grateful to my wife Shirley and our children, Rachael and Nathan, who have been extremely support-

ive of this project, and have continually encouraged me during
the writing of this book.

Finally, to all those many, many people who have been either
a Barnabas, a Paul, or a Timothy in my life, I am more grateful
than these meager words can express. To each of you goes not
only my thanks for so many warm memories, but also my love
and affection.

RON LEE DAVIS

"Years ago, before seminaries existed, future ministers were
trained by sitting under the mentorship of pastors, studying the
Scriptures with them and working alongside them. Now this
process is available to lay people through the mentoring relationship. I believe that there is no more significant ministry for
gifted pastors and strong churches than to mentor younger
Christians in their daily walk. The message of Ron's book may
be the best hope for the future of the church in the 21st century."

Bruce Larson
Author and Co-Pastor
Crystal Cathedral

"This book grabs me. It is fresh, practical, challenging—and
unusual. It is all but impossible to read this book without getting caught up in the strategy of Jesus. Ron Davis is one of the
best writers in the Christian world. He knows how to paint a
picture with words that any of us can understand. I not only
recommend this book, but urge every believer to read it."

Ben Haden
Speaker
"Changed Lives" TV-Radio

"Ron's newest book challenges me to a greater understanding of the importance of mentoring in the Christian life. As a result of this book, I clearly see the need of mentors in my own life, as well as the urgency of becoming a mentor to others. Ron's powerful call to integrity, devotion and courageous endurance will penetrate the heart of every believer. This is a must-read!"

> **Dave Dravecky**
> *Author of* Comeback *and*
> *Former Star Pitcher*
> *San Francisco Giants baseball team*

"Ron Lee Davis has again put his finger on our pulse and helped us discover practical ways whereby we can become more Christlike. He shows us how we can pass our biblical values on to future generations. In my own life, the mentoring process has made a profound impact. Davis' deep wisdom is hard-earned. This book is a winner! I hope it inspires countless new mentoring relationships for the kingdom!"

> **Tim Hansel**
> *Author of* You Gotta Keep Dancin
> *and* Holy Sweat

"I have read a number of excellent books by Ron Lee Davis. I believe this is his best yet! He convinced me that mentoring is important; he surprised me with any number of unexpected insights, and time and time again he caught me emotionally. I immediately invited Ron to be a guest on the 'Chapel of the Air' broadcast."

> **David Mains**
> *Author and Director*
> *"The Chapel of the Air"*

"Ron Davis has produced a clear guide to successful mentoring. It is both biblical and eminently practical. Tough problems are explored and workable remedies suggested. Highly recommended to any who tries to work closely with others."

Ray Stedman
Author and Pastor Emeritus
Peninsula Bible Church
Palo Alto, California

"In his book *Mentoring: The Strategy of the Master,* Ron Davis has illuminated for us an essential biblical pattern that is sorely needed in our day. In a style that is clear, inspiring, and replete with real-life examples, Ron not only describes biblical mentoring, but also offers very helpful and practical ideas as to how we might incorporate this pattern in our own lives."

Jeff Siemon
Former All-Pro Linebacker
Minnesota Vikings football team

"Modeling, motivating, and mentoring are much more than buzz words. They are absolute necessities in a world of aimlessness and hopelessness. Ron Lee Davis puts bite into the buzz and the result is a readable, sensitive, helpful book."

Jill Briscoe
International Speaker and Author

"Ron Davis is one of the most creative pastors in America. He has all the accoutrements of a successful church leader. But more than his able mind, excellent training, and broad experience, he lives in depth. He has allowed God to speak to him personally in what he seeks to communicate. He is a communicator of grace."

Lloyd John Ogilvie
Senior Pastor
First Presbyterian Church
Hollywood, California

"I am deeply grateful for this in-depth, practical study. Having written on this theme, I am most pleased to note how my friend Ron Lee Davis complements and supplements so beautifully what I have sought to say, in a moving, warm, and compassionate manner. This is a study which will invigorate, challenge, and inspire any and all who will seek to follow in the footsteps of our Lord in this key role of biblical discipleship. I recommend it without reservation."

Ted W. Engstrom
President Emeritus, World Vision
Author of The Fine Art of Mentoring

"In a day characterized by 'living for yourself,' Ron Lee Davis comes along to challenge that image. He presents a practical, easy-to-read handbook on how to share your life with others. Through this process we learn to live for the next generation. Be careful—this book is subtle. It will quietly change your outlook on life!"

Bill Butterworth
Speaker and Author

"Congratulations to Ron Lee Davis for his exploration of this crucial and timely subject."

Anne Ortlund
Speaker and Author

"Ron Lee Davis has not forgotten that discipleship is a relationship, not a program. This is a manual written by a man who is both a mentor and a protege! Ron shares with us the invaluable insight of a realist who knows both the joys and disappointments of mentoring. He writes in a practical style so that the reader does not have to be either a rocket-scientist or a professional saint to begin a lifestyle of mentoring and learning from others.

"This is a book chock-full of practical insight and wisdom in one of the most important yet overlooked areas in the church today. It is a must for anyone who wants to become so infected with spirituality that he or she becomes a dangerous carrier, spreading the virus of God's kingdom for eternal impact."

Howard G. Hendricks
Chairman
Center for Christian Leadership
Distinguished Professor
Dallas Theological Seminary

"Through spiritual, historical, and deeply scriptural examples, Ron Lee Davis brings to life the mentoring process. 'Making a crucial investment in another person's life' is the powerful truth he teaches as he shares the process of 'passing on a rich heritage and faith.' Never a more timely, impacting, and thorough book for today's Christian community."

Carolyn Koons
Author of Beyond Betrayal